ACKNOWLEDGEMENTS

When you see a little boy defeating a mighty man, you must know that there is an unseen source giving support to the boy. When you see a river flowing up-hill you should realize that a certain force is pushing it. Whenever you discover an ordinary person doing extraordinary things you must know that there is unseen source supplying strength to the person.

I want to acknowledge the inspiration from the Holy-Spirit that moved me to write this book. Without the touch of the Holy-Spirit this book would have remained only a figment of my imagination without any manifestation. I am indeed very grateful to the Holy-Spirit for his wonderful support and motivation.

I would like to acknowledge the immense encouragement from my wife, Felicia Ebunlomo. She was always positive and supportive during the period of writing this book. She has been a channel through which Almighty God has been moulding me through life.

My two sons, Daniel and David, have been wonderful and I am indeed very grateful to them.

I acknowledge, with an immense appreciation, the works of the following people in editing this book: Mr Mayowa Peters, Mr Adeyemi Adeniyi, Mr Adeyemi Bukola, and Ms Ehime Ayeni.

Finally, my heartfelt thanks to the entire members of The Redeemed Christian Church of God, Glory of God Parish, Bristol, England, for being a good family of God to me and my home. God bless you all in Jesus name. Amen!

INTRODUCTION

A Journey is the act of going from one place to another. It usually has a starting point with a desired destination. Life is about journeys; it involves series of movement from one location to another.

This book is about a journey but a unique type. It is about progress. It is about desire not to remain in one position. God is a God of progress. God wants his children to advance in every facet of their lives. As you read this book you will discover that it is very imperative for you not to be complacent. You must strive to advance in every area of your life because this will give glory to the name of God.

The Journey to the Next Level will also educate you about things that hinder progress and it will enlighten you to discover how character faults can frustrate destiny.

Nevertheless, for every problem there is a solution. This book will educate you on how to overcome the difficulties on the way to the next level. You will discover in this book that strength is available to complete your journey.

> **1 JOHN 4:4**
>
> Ye are of God, little children, and have overcome them: because greater is he that is in you, than he that is in the world.

The above Bible verse indicates that you are an overcomer. There is nothing that can hinder your journey unless you quit. There is no mountain too big for you to climb. There is no giant too huge that you can't defeat. You will discover in this book that you are stronger than you think. With God on your side you can go very far in the journey of life.

It is time for you to take the journey to the next level in your job, ministry, career, business etc.

It is my prayer that as you read this book your spirit man will be empowered such that you will mount wings as eagles to fly to the next level in every segment of your life in Jesus name. See you on top!

CONTENTS

1 Beyond the Sky 9

2 The Helpers 17

3 Divine Guidance 31

4 Holes in the Armour 45

5 Journey in Stages 65

6 Strength for the Journey 79

7 Press On 101

Final Word 111

Prayer 113

CHAPTER 1

BEYOND THE SKY

In the beginning, God put man in the Garden of Eden to work it. After the fall of man, God sent man out of the garden. Since then, man has been spreading over the surface of the earth. Man has become a goal-seeking creature. No man was designed to live in stagnancy. Man is naturally a progressive being.

According to the old adage: 'The sky is the limit.' Today man has gone deeper into the journey of discoveries; the sky is no longer the limit. Man has gone beyond the sky and then explored further into the realm of galaxies. Have you set the sky as your limit? Never allow stagnancy in any area of your life. The reason you were elevated to your present level was to give you a ladder to climb to the next level. Until you get to Heaven, the final destination for Christians, never stop rising. Three different scenarios shall be considered in this chapter to give the understanding that Christians should always aspire to look beyond their present level of achievements.

BEYOND HOREB

> **DEUTERONOMY 1:6-8**
>
> The Lord our God spake unto us in Horeb, saying, Ye have dwelt long enough in this mount:
>
> Turn you, and take your journey, and go to the mount of the Amorites, and unto all the places nigh thereunto, in the plain, in the hills, and in the vale, and in the south, and by the sea side, to the land of the Canaanites, and unto Lebanon, unto the great river, the river Euphrates.
>
> Behold, I have set the land before you: go in and possess the land which the Lord sware unto your fathers, Abraham, Isaac, and Jacob, to give unto them and to their seed after them.

Horeb was the place where God first appeared to Moses in *Exodus 3:1*. God told Moses in *Exodus 3:12* that when the Israelites are delivered out of Egypt they would serve God on this mountain. To fulfil this word from God, the Israelites eventually came to mount Horeb: - a place where they worshipped God. Though, this had come to fulfilment it was not their final destination. They had been brought to Mount Horeb in order to further their journey. According to the above passage part of their inheritance was waiting for them to possess it. God had to tell them that they had stayed too long at the mountain; the land of their inheritance was waiting to be claimed. Many Christians have come to their Mount Horeb and the fulfilment they are experiencing there is making them stay too long at this place such that they have forgotten advancement. Many have turned temporary dwelling place to their permanent place of stay.

The comfort and fulfilment at Horeb may deceive many Christians to develop a sense of great achievement and unknowingly the devil can tie them down. It is time to aspire to move to the next level. It is true God has brought you to where you are presently but did He tell you that you have reached your final destination? Majority of individuals are locked up in their comfort zone and, as such, are unable to progress to the next level.

BEYOND POTIPHAR'S HOUSE

> **GENESIS 39:1-9**
>
> And Joseph was brought down to Egypt; and Potiphar, an officer of Pharaoh, captain of the guard, an Egyptian, bought him of the hands of the Ishmaelites, which had brought him down thither.
>
> And the Lord was with Joseph, and he was a prosperous man; and he was in the house of his master the Egyptian. And his master saw that the Lord was with him, and that the Lord made all that he did to prosper in his hand. And Joseph found grace in his sight, and he served him: and he made him overseer over his house, and all that he had he put into his hand.
>
> And it came to pass from the time that he had made him overseer in his house, and over all that he had, that the Lord blessed the Egyptian's house for Joseph's sake; and the blessing of the Lord was upon all that he had in the house, and in the field.

> And he left all that he had in Joseph's hand; and he knew not ought he had, save the bread which he did eat. And Joseph was a goodly person, and well favoured.
>
> And it came to pass after these things, that his master's wife cast her eyes upon Joseph; and she said, Lie with me. But he refused, and said unto his master's wife, Behold, my master wotteth not what is with me in the house, and he hath committed all that he hath to my hand; There is none greater in this house than I; neither hath he kept back any thing from me but thee, because thou art his wife: how then can I do this great wickedness, and sin against God?

Joseph had dreams of greatness. In *Genesis 37:6-11* it was revealed to him that he was born to be great; but the time and location were kept secret from him. He had no idea of the time and place of fulfilment of this dream. The above bible passage revealed Joseph's life at Portiphar's house. The Lord was with Joseph. That is, Joseph carried God's presence even as a slave in Portiphar's house. Furthermore, Joseph became an overseer in Portiphar's house ruling over Portiphar's possession. That is, at Portiphar's house Joseph was the second in command after Potiphar. This could be likened to the position of a prime minister. What a success in a foreign land! After sometime Mrs Potiphar proposed love affairs to Joseph. The Devil would have interpreted this situation to Joseph as an opportunity to fortify his stay in Portiphar's house. With Mrs. Potiphar on his side, the sky would be Joseph's limit in that house. He would be able to do as he pleased. Mrs. Potiphar would no doubt lure her husband to grant more authority to Joseph. Probably the greatness God revealed to Joseph in the past had come into fulfilment in this place. The Devil is a liar. At this stage Joseph had no idea of the future but yet, he looked beyond the 'sky'. He looked beyond Portiphar's House. He didn't allow himself to be deceived by the devil's promise. The fear of God in him enabled him to say 'NO' to the enemy's proposal. There are so many individuals destined to rule nations but because of greed and lack of self-control are ruling a few individuals. Even where they are presently, they will soon be kicked out because the positions they occupy are not from God. Blessed are you if you are able to look beyond your present level of achievement. You can do better. You can go further if you can think further. You are not a success, until God calls you a success. So until God calls you a success never stop rising. It is time for you to go to the next level. Don't stop here, you are on a journey.

BEYOND GOLIATH

1 SAMUEL 17:48-51

And it came to pass, when the Philistine arose, and came and drew nigh to meet David, that David hasted, and ran toward the army to meet the Philistine.

And David put his hand in his bag, and took thence a stone, and slang it, and smote the Philistine in his forehead, that the stone sunk into his forehead; and he fell upon his face to the earth.

So David prevailed over the Philistine with a sling and with a stone, and smote the Philistine, and slew him; but there was no sword in the hand of David.

> Therefore David ran, and stood upon the Philistine, and took his sword, and drew it out of the sheath thereof, and slew him, and cut off his head therewith. And when the Philistines saw their champion was dead, they fled.

In the above passage, David prevailed over Goliath. The consequences of this success are -

1. According to *1 Samuel 18:5-7*, David became the commander of the army. He had been identified as a man of war. The success over Goliath advertised his capability and potential. He was promoted to the leadership position in Israel.

2. David became a national hero. Everybody's heart was with him. People accepted him. They embraced him as their deliverer. He came out of obscurity into the light. People started to celebrate him. Fame and praise came to David. David's popularity increased in the land.

3. According to *1 Samuel 17:25-27*, David became a man of blessing after killing Goliath. The reward of killing Goliath was substantial to enrich David. It is clear from the above that killing Goliath had indeed promoted David, but did this indicate the full package of promotion for David from God?

According to *1 Samuel 16:1-13*, David was destined to be King of Israel. Therefore whatever success he may have recorded for killing Goliath was transitional not final. It was a shadow of what was coming not the real thing. David was not carried away by the success of killing Goliath, but he was looking for the day he would possess his real possession. Many Christians have only killed Goliath but have not ruled as kings though they are destined to be kings.

The success of killing Goliath has made many people to assume wrongly that they have reached the final destination of their journey of progress on earth. They think they have got the best from God. While they are rejoicing that they have arrived at the final destination, heaven is actually mourning because better positions are anxiously waiting for their arrival but to no avail. Beloved, though you have killed Goliath, you can still be king and until then, never relent. It is time for you to come out of complacent imprisonment. It creates fake satisfaction and can rob you of future blessings. It is time to go to the next level. You need to come out of your shell, and until you have a personal conviction that you have not reached your final destination, you will not be able to aspire for greater success. You need to recognise the existence of your self-created mental prisons. You also need to be ready to break out of these mental prisons.

Many Christians have become mental midgets because they have stayed too long in a place as they see no reason to search for further advancement. They have indirectly placed a ceiling over their lives, so every touch of the Holy Spirit to wake them up to move to the next level is resisted. According to *Romans 5:17*, Christians were destined to reign in life with Jesus Christ. You can't reign in life when you get carried away with little successes and no longer value further advancement. May God empower you to desire further advancement and progress in Jesus name.

Amen. When you develop wrong beliefs concerning God's purpose for your life you may end up with wrong attitudes that are capable of keeping you in one place longer than necessary. Therefore, your expectations and attitude associated with your thoughts are dictated by your beliefs and consequently influence your actions. May your thoughts and actions be in obedience to the purpose of God for your life. Amen.

PRAYER

The Lord Jesus open my eyes of understanding to see your wonderful purpose for my life and help me to embrace it.

Every self imposed limitation in my life, Father deliver me from it today in Jesus name. I reject every lie of the enemy concerning my life in Jesus name.

Father make me wiser than my opposers in Jesus name. Every power designed to keep me stagnant is broken today in Jesus name.

The grace to resist the devil in all areas of my life I receive it today in Jesus name. The anointing to breakthrough every manner of demonic constraint over my life I receive it today in Jesus name.

Every negative force interfering with my thinking patterns be broken today in Jesus name.

The Lord Jesus help me to excel in all my ways. Father destroy every demonic control over my destiny in Jesus name.

CHAPTER 2

THE HELPERS

A helper is someone that does something for the benefit of somebody in need. Human helpers are organised by God for His children's assistance. God organises helpers for His children for the fulfilment of their destinies. It is very important for you to understand that your destiny is connected to that of others God had created .That is, you can't operate in isolation. This calls for development of the ability to relate well with people. Therefore your journey to the next level will require helpers. There are various reasons why God organises helpers for you and these include:

1. God-given assignment or blessing is always greater than the recipient; so the person needs assistance.

2. There will be a time when the enemy will rise to test your purpose whether it is of God or of man. This is the time of challenges. The person needs a "burden sharer". God- given helpers will be available to share the burdens and challenges of the journey with you.

3. God wants to raise an army through you. God wants to raise a formidable team of winners that will be able to stand against the kingdom of darkness. So He will bring you helpers to form a team with you so that together you will be strong. A soldier can chase few but an army can chase many. Spiritual warfare isn't a battle of one person but of a combination of united soldiers.

4. God wants to produce a network of winners. Those that God will bring to help you in your journey to the next level may be reposted tomorrow after they have achieved their mission in your life. In their new location, they also continue with their own God-given mission and God brings helpers into their own lives too. This chain continues to be built up. Since the past has linked you together then you continue like that and remember each other and relate together as friends. This is a network of winners.

CASE STUDIES

We shall consider few cases from the Bible where God made helpers available for his vessels.

Adam and Eve

GENESIS 2:15-22

And the Lord God took the man, and put him into the garden of Eden to dress it and to keep it. And the Lord God commanded the man, saying, Of every tree of the garden thou mayest freely eat: But of the tree of the

> knowledge of good and evil, thou shalt not eat of it: for in the day that thou eatest thereof thou shalt surely die.
>
> And the Lord God said, It is not good that the man should be alone; I will make him an help meet for him. And out of the ground the Lord God formed every beast of the field, and every fowl of the air; and brought them unto Adam to see what he would call them: and whatsoever Adam called every living creature, that was the name thereof.
>
> And Adam gave names to all cattle, and to the fowl of the air, and to every beast of the field; but for Adam there was not found an help meet for him. And the Lord God caused a deep sleep to fall upon Adam and he slept: and he took one of his ribs, and closed up the flesh instead thereof; And the rib, which the Lord God had taken from man, made he a woman, and brought her unto the man.

In this situation, God had put Adam in the Garden of Eden to tend and keep it. Due to this assignment, some needs arose in Adam's life and it needed someone of relevant qualities and attributes. In this situation not just anybody could fit into Adam's assignment but it had to be a person who could fill the vacuum. The person had to be of a very similar attribute to Adam. So, Adam needed a helper who would not be of strange characteristics. Every helper has got certain role to play. Eve came into Adam's life to help him for daily work, procreation and support. Therefore, as God is bringing helpers into your life you need to discover their roles in your journey.

Please note that Adam didn't seek a helper by himself but God did. This means that it is God that knows better who can adequately fit into your situation. Adam didn't put himself in the garden but God did. Therefore God knew the situation of Adam better than Adam. If the assignment you are doing originated from God then it is God's responsibility, not yours to organise helpers for you. It should also be noted that God didn't provide a suitable helper for Adam the same day he was put in the garden. At the beginning of his journey in the garden he started it alone and later things started falling into places. The timing is of God. For every stage of your journey, God knows your needs and arrangement has been provided. As you take a step of faith alone to move to the next level, at an appropriate time, things will begin to fall into place on their own accord. May God stir up your spirit to trust Him for your daily provision. Amen.

Moses and Aaron

EXODUS 4:10-16

And Moses said unto the Lord, O my Lord, I am not eloquent, neither heretofore, nor since thou hast spoken unto thy servant: but I am slow of speech, and of a slow tongue.

And the Lord said unto him, Who hath made man's mouth? or who maketh the dumb, or deaf, or the seeing, or the blind? have not I the Lord?

Now therefore go, and I will be with thy mouth, and teach thee what thou shalt say.

> And he said, O my Lord, send, I pray thee, by the hand of him whom thou wilt send.
>
> And the anger of the Lord was kindled against Moses, and he said, Is not Aaron the Levite thy brother? I know that he can speak well. And also, behold, he cometh forth to meet thee: and when he seeth thee, he will be glad in his heart.
>
> And thou shalt speak unto him, and put words in his mouth: and I will be with thy mouth, and with his mouth, and will teach you what ye shall do.
>
> And he shall be thy spokesman unto the people: and he shall be, even he shall be to thee instead of a mouth, and thou shalt be to him instead of God.

God called Moses into his ministry. It was time for Moses to move to the next level of his journey on earth. Moses had limitation-inability to speak well. He needed a helper that would prevent his limitation from affecting his ministry negatively. Moses reminded God of his limitation and considered himself unfit for the assignment. Instead of Moses to realise the need to ask for a helper, he disqualified himself. The conviction you have that you aren't able to do the work God has given you is an indication that it is from God but not a final judgement that you are unfit.

The requirements needed by you for your journey to the next level are the responsibilities of God, not yours. In Isaiah 50:7, it is stated that God will make help available. That is, God knows your limitation before he drops certain plans into your mind. Therefore, trust God for helpers. It should also be noted that before Moses complained of his limitation, God had already made provision for a helper - *Exodus 4:14*. God had already placed his hand on Aaron to come to Moses on his own accord. God said Aaron would be glad to help Moses. It is God that tunes the heart of a man to serve another man. When people refuse to serve you, don't force them, it's because God hasn't tuned their hearts to do so.

In *Proverbs 21:1*, it is stated that the heart of the king is under the control of God. If God can tune the heart of a king what about his subordinates? God can tune anyone's heart. It should also be noted that the role of a helper is spelt out by God in *Exodus 4:15-16* - Moses' mouth-piece. In your journey to the next level you must identify the role of the helper God is bringing into your life. This will create orderliness and help you to identify the needs for more helpers.

It is important for you to be aware that you don't have any limitation that is capable of preventing you from fulfilling your purpose. Your physical disability, family background, hatred and other limitations you can think of are not capable of limiting your journey to the next level. If you are willing, God is ready. In fact, your limitation is an opportunity for God to glorify Himself in your life.

A lady was born crippled. She went for an interview for a job with able people. After the interview, the Board of the organisation met to discuss about whom to appoint. They agreed to give the job to the lady. Their argument was that other candidates are physically able to search for job elsewhere but the crippled lady has limitation that will not enable her to move around in search of job. So, the crippled lady was given the job. God used her limitation as a reason to favour her.

As you are reading this book, all the limitations in your life shall be used by God to promote you to the next level. Your limitation shall become a stepping-stone to a higher ground in Jesus name. Arise and let your light shine.

Rahab and the spies

> **JOSHUA 2:1-6**
>
> And Joshua the son of Nun sent out of Shittim two men to spy secretly, saying, Go view the land, even Jericho. And they went, and came into an harlot's house, named Rahab, and lodged there.
>
> And it was told the king of Jericho, saying, Behold, there came men in hither to night of the children of Israel to search out the country.
>
> And the king of Jericho sent unto Rahab, saying, Bring forth the men that are come to thee, which are entered into thine house: for they be come to search out all the country.
>
> And the woman took the two men, and hid them, and said thus, There came men unto me, but I wist not whence they were: And it came to pass about the time of shutting of the gate, when it was dark, that the men went out: whither the men went I wot not: pursue after them quickly; for ye shall overtake them.

> But she had brought them up to the roof of the house, and hid them with the stalks of flax, which she had laid in order upon the roof.

Here the Israelites were to take Jericho by force. It is extremely dangerous to invade a territory without necessary information. The spies were sent to the land. They knew no one in Jericho, but God created Jericho and the people living there. Before they reached Jericho, God had already gone ahead of the spies to arrange a helper for them. In the midst of the enemies, God still organised a suitable helper. Rehab was so willing to do whatever was necessary in order to enable the spies to achieve their mission. God, in His power, sovereignly led the spies to the right place. *Psalm 37:23* states that the steps of a good man are ordered by God. When God is in control of your steps, He leads you to people whose hearts He has prepared to help you. Let it be known that Jericho was filled with evil people including Rehab. If the spies had entered Jericho with the belief that there was no good person in the land, they could have missed the help of Rahab and that would have made their mission difficult.

It is important for you not to pollute your mind towards people because you don't know who God will use. A wrong mindset will rob you of receiving assistance from people. Let your mind be filled with good thoughts about people. Favour comes to a prepared mind. When you approach people or situations with a negative attitude you have closed the door of your mind against any benefit you ought to enjoy from them. Even in the midst of your enemies,

God can raise a helper for you. It should be noted that the role of Rahab was to give the spies accommodation, not to be involved in the spying scenario.

Every helper has a definite role to play. *Joshua 2:8-11* reveals that Rahab had heard about the Israelites even before the spies came. God had relayed the information about the Israelites to Rahab and this might have contributed to her willingness to help the spies. If no one is ready to help you, it maybe because they have heard information about your bad reputation. When people hear that all the people that have had an encounter with you regret knowing you, then you must expect isolation. No one wants to get associated with a failure and morally bankrupt person. If you have record of series of failures in business, ministry or other life endeavour, people will approach you with caution. Also, *Joshua 2:12-14* reveals the deal between Rahab and the spies. In *Joshua 6:25* the deal was fulfilled. The Israelites paid favour for favour. The entire family of Rehab was spared. This action of the Israelites was very significant concerning their future.

> **PROVERBS 17:13**
>
> Whoso rewardeth evil for good, evil shall not depart from his house.

If the Israelites had rewarded Rahab evil for the good she did to them, it would have prevented future helper from coming their way. The journey of life is in stages and people you met in a stage, you may come across them in another stage. Also spiritually, it states that evil shouldn't be paid for good. So if no one come to help you at this stage of your life, it maybe that you have paid evil for good to former helpers. God has given many people an assignment but they are struggling alone. It maybe because they have violated some aspects of spiritual laws. Beware, your past may haunt you. May God's mercy prevail over judgement in your life in Jesus name. May the blood of Jesus silence your accusers' voice in Jesus name.

David Builds His Army

1 CHRONICLES 12:18-22

Then the spirit came upon Amasai, who was chief of the captains, and he said, Thine are we, David, and on thy side, thou son of Jesse: peace, peace be unto thee, and peace be to thine helpers; for thy God helpeth thee. Then David received them, and made them captains of the band. And there fell some of Manasseh to David, when he came with the Philistines against Saul to battle: but they helped them not: for the lords of the Philistines upon advisement sent him away, saying, He will fall to his master Saul to the jeopardy of our heads.

As he went to Ziklag, there fell to him of Manasseh, Adnah, and Jozabad, and Jediael, and Michael, and Jozabad, and Elihu, and Zilthai, captains of the thousands that were of Manasseh. And they helped David against the band of the rovers: for they were all mighty men of valour, and were captains in the host For at that time day by day there came to David to help him, until it was a great host, like the host of God.

THE HELPERS

David was anointed to rule over the house of Israel. He was to deliver the Israelites from their enemies and ensure their security. David had to build an army for battle so as to fulfil his calling. When David was anointed in *1 Samuel 16:13*, he had no understanding of the bigness of his calling; but God knew all the details.

At the appointed time, people came to help David on their own accord. The helpers that came were suitable ones, with ability to fight war. They were mighty men of valour. God who appointed David knew the calibre of people David would need as helpers. If those that came to help you could not fit properly into your journey, it maybe that you were the one who influenced them to be your helper, not God. God will always provide suitable helpers. It should also be noted that majority of those that came to help David had already served King Saul before. They were the people that might have been used against David in the past. Many people that hate you today may be doing so because of negative influence they are receiving from someone elsewhere. When the source of such negative influence is removed by God, the same people may come to help you tomorrow. Never rule out the possibility of somebody serving you tomorrow. The enemies of today may become close associates tomorrow.

It should be observed that the whole scenario was organised by the Spirit of God (*1 Chronicles 12:18*). It wasn't an idea of David. David as a human being had no power to influence such a crowd to his side. When the helpers came, all the vacant positions were filled; and David was able to build an army.

On your journey to the next level, there will be a need for helpers of different calibre. If the purpose is of God, He will bring able helpers. If you have a suspicion spirit, you may find it difficult to accommodate some helpers in your journey. If David allowed flesh to rule his mind, he would have been suspicious of those that God brought to help him. Many have sent their helpers away because they suspect they are linked with their former enemies. A man of unforgiving spirit will use his own hand to send his helpers away and end up blaming other people instead of himself. You must also know that you can't dictate to God whom He should bring as helpers. You should be ready to move on in life with whoever God decides to bring to help you. God didn't consult David for approval and David didn't question God. God doesn't promote enmity. He can bring anybody to help you and you must accommodate the person. David put helpers in position according to their skills and past record. They were people of different skills and experiences.

You must have relevant information about the helpers God brings to you so that you will not wrongly place them. When people are given an assignment they haven't being trained for, they become dissatisfied and rebel. Many leaders have produced rebellious helpers because they were wrongly placed. If you have a helper that frustrates your mission, it maybe because of wrong placement. An army of helpers come to help and stay permanently as long as God wants. May God build an army of helpers for you in Jesus name. Every source that is influencing people against you shall dry up in Jesus name. Amen.

> **PSALM 33:20**
>
> Our soul waiteth for the Lord: he is our help and our shield.

It is God that provides helpers; not man. The following hints may help you to identify God's sent helpers.

1. The helper renders the help without putting his selfish interest forward. God will not send you a helper that will demand bribe before rendering the assistance. If it is of God, you will not need to violate God's rule before receiving help from men. You don't need to buy someone's conscience in order to receive help but after you have received help you need to show a sign of appreciation. Never pay evil for good. Pay good for good done to you.

2. The helpers serve and not to boss. The helpers brought by God will not hijack the headship from you. Eve came to help Adam but Adam remained the head. However, if the leader does not show leadership ability, the followers may be tempted by the Devil to hijack his office. Since you are the carrier of your destiny, whoever comes to help you must be ready to operate under your guidance.

3. The helpers from God will show willingness to help, because the hand of God will be upon them for your sake. So you don't need to influence anybody to help you. You don't need to convince people to help you,

God will do that. If you succeed to influence anybody to help you, such a person will only give his body not the heart, and soon, he will get tired of you.

PRAYER

Father, let everything you have created co-operate with my destiny in Jesus name.

If there is anything in me, capable of frustrating helpers from locating me, the lord Jesus remove it from my life today.

Father, open my eyes to recognise the move of your Spirit in my life in Jesus name.

Father, angels among human beings (capable of doing me favour) direct them to me by your power in Jesus name.

Father, help me to build and maintain constructive relationship with people in Jesus name.

Every mark of hatred in my life, I wash you away by the blood of Jesus.

Every power fashioned to sponsor failure in my journey, I paralyse you today in Jesus name.

Father, let your favour rest upon my life, in Jesus name.

Father, make me an undefeatable soldier in your kingdom in Jesus name.

Father, help me to breakthrough in all my struggles in Jesus name.

CHAPTER 3

DIVINE GUIDANCE

Guidance is the act of showing the way and direction. It involves help, advice or instruction usually from someone who is more qualified. When God shows up in the journey of your life, He leads you to your destination by His power. It is written in *Psalm 75:6-7* that exaltation comes neither from the east nor west nor south but from God. That is, the promotion you are seeking is only found in the Lord. Therefore, it is a wise thing to allow God to guide you in your journey to the next level. Moreover, it is also stated in the word of God (*John 3:27*) that a man can receive nothing unless it has been given to him from heaven. This indicates that the promotion and better life you are seeking can only be obtained from Heaven. Therefore, heaven needs to be involved in your journey.

WHEN GOD GUIDES YOU

When God guides you, the benefits are wonderful and many. Let us examine some of them:

He Plans Your Route

There is a road that leads to success without being worn out. God is a route planner and when He is allowed to do it, you are sure of reaching your destination.

> **ISAIAH 48:17**
>
> Thus saith the Lord, thy Redeemer, the Holy One of Israel; I am the Lord thy God which teacheth thee to profit, which leadeth thee by the way that thou shouldest go.

That is, God knows the best route that can take you to your destination. He can lead you the way you should go. This means God has to be in front while you, follow His foot steps. If you want Him to lead you then you have to surrender leadership of your journey to him.

> **Exodus 13:17-18**
>
> And it came to pass, when Pharaoh had let the people go, that God led them not through the way of the land of the Philistines, although that was near; for God said, Lest peradventure the people repent when they see war, and they return to Egypt:
>
> But God led the people about, through the way of the wilderness of the Red sea: and the children of Israel went up harnnessed out of the land of Egypt.

God planned the route for the Israelites on their way to the Promised Land. God knows the best route to follows. God decided to take them through the longer route because if they should follow a shorter one, they would face battle so early and at this stage, they had not been trained for battle. So, God considered their ability, exposure and challenges ahead to decide the route they would follow. In your journey to the next level, there may be a route that seems shorter and faster but the challenges on the way may be overwhelming and this may make God to decide a route that is longer but safer for you. Though there may still be a battle to fight on the way, but it will come at an appropriate time. God will not let you fight a battle that He hasn't trained you for. Therefore, if you find yourself facing battle that overcome you, it is an indication that God wasn't leading you. He hasn't planned the route for you. Probably, you decided on the route yourself.

He Orders Your Steps

That is God is the designer of steps that can lead a man to his inheritance.

> **PSALM 37:23**
>
> The steps of a good man are ordered by the Lord: and he delighteth in his way.

Since God plans the route then He knows the way to go. When God orders your steps, He upholds you with His hand such that though you may fall but you will never be cast down. He leads you, according to his good purpose. He controls, directs and manages your footsteps. If you need a helper, God leads such that you will be in contact with the helper. Your steps will not be misdirected. The Israelites had never been to the Promised Land before. So they needed God to order their steps. It was God that ordered their steps through the wilderness until they reached their final destination. If your journey to the next level is aborted or comes to an abrupt end, it means God hasn't been ordering your steps. God ensures you get to every stage at the right time. A picture of how God orders the steps of a righteous man is seen in *1 Samuel 30:1-17*. In this scenario David and his men came to Ziklag and discovered that the Amalekites had invaded their homes. There was a need to pursue the enemies but before they did that, David consulted God for direction and God told him to pursue the enemy. God ordered their steps such that they met an Egyptian man who helped them to locate the identity of the raiders. (*1 Samuel 30:11*). When God orders your steps, you will get to every stage at the right time. You will not miss your helper. Everything will be divinely orchestrated.

He Manages Your Speed

When God guides you, He controls your speed, and makes it appropriate such that you will neither be too fast or too slow. Some people are slow runners and if God is not their guide, they may become late achievers in life. Many have a long record of wasted years because their pace is too slow for their destiny. Unless God manages your speed, you will not be able to arrive at every stage of your journey at the right time. Speed and direction are of God. When God is the guide, He can accelerate your journey. A man on a mission can't play with speed. In *Acts 8:39-40*, Phillip was on a mission and by human strength he could not have got to the next location at the right time. Timing is important in achieving one's divine purpose. Hence, the spirit of the Lord transported him to the next location. In *1 Samuel 2:9*, it is written that by strength shall no man prevail. God wants to control your speed and strength. If your strength can't match the required speed to get to every stage of your journey at the right time, God will supernaturally work it out. When God is your guide, your limitation has no effect. In *1 Kings 18:45-46*, Ahab was long gone (using human strength and speed) but within the twinkling of an eye, Elijah overtook him because God's hand came upon Elijah. If you are always late for an appointment or you can't match the speed required for your race of breakthrough, then you need to invite God to be in control of your speed.

He Gives You Counsel

When God is your guide, He equips you with wisdom that will enable you to outwit your enemies.

> **PROVERB 15:22**
>
> Without counsel purposes are disappointed: but in the multitude of counsellers they are established.

In essence, success can only be achieved when a man receives proper counsel. When you receive counsel from God you are sure of victory because *Isaiah 46:10* says His counsel will always stand. God knows the strength and weakness of your situation. He knows the challenges on your journey to the next level, so He is able to equip you with counsel to outwit your opposers. Your journey to the next level needs proper planning and counsel is also required to establish it.

When your plans fail, it may be due to lack of counsel from God. When nothing works out well, it may be because you walk in your own counsel. When you are confused and don't know the way forward, it may be because you haven't acknowledged that counsel from God is the only sure route to success.

> **JAMES 1:5**
>
> If any of you lack wisdom, let him ask of God, that giveth to all men liberally, and upbraideth not; and it shall be given him.

So, learn how to ask for wisdom from God. Seek His counsel and you will get to the next level. *Proverbs 3:7* states that you should never be wise in your own eyes. That is, don't walk in your own opinion. The next level you are going to is a new position because you have never been there before. Therefore you need God who knows all things even before they came to existence.

He Encourages You

Journey to the next level entails passing through difficult situation. When God becomes your guide, He gives encouragement so that you will not abandon the journey.

> **ZECHARIAH 4:9**
>
> The hands of Zerubbabel have laid the foundation of this house; his hands shall also finish it; and thou shalt know that the Lord of hosts hath sent me unto you.

Zerubbabel, having laid the foundation of the temple, was about to succumb to discouragement by abandoning the completion of the temple; but God came with a word of encouragement to enable them to see God's ability to give grace and empower their souls. God can encourage you by sending words of hope to you. Also, *Haggai 1:14* states that God stirred up the spirit of Zerubbabel, that of Joshua the high priest and that of the remnant of the people. This is the direct action of God to work on cold hearts for renewal of desire. This renews their energy. When God is your guide, He strengthens your spirit such that a source of discouragement becomes a source of motivation. When God opens your eyes to see the gain of getting to the next level, it motivates you not to abandon the journey.

He Shows Up In Your Crisis

Enemy is always afraid of your success; so he orchestrates series of storms to prevent your advancement; but when God is your guide, He shows up in crisis. When God shows up in your crisis:

1. He delivers you out if it. *2 Samuel 22:17-18* states that God rescued David from all his enemies because He has become his guide.

2. He quenches the crisis by removing the instrument of it. *2 Samuel 22:1* states that God delivered David from the hand of Saul. Saul was the major instrument of crisis facing David. When God removed Saul, the major crisis in David's life ended. When God is your guide, He eliminates the instrument of your crisis so that you can proceed with your journey to the next level. When you find yourself being entangled in crisis on your journey to the next level, probably you have ignored God's guidance. God will not allow His people to be consumed as stated in *Lamentations 3:22*.

CONDITIONS FOR GOD'S GUIDANCE

God is ready to guide you to reach the next level; nevertheless this will depend on the conditions such as:

Operating in God's Purpose

Your plan must be in the purpose of God for your life. Your vision and dream must be according to God's purpose. God will not finance the project of another man.

> **EPHESIANS 1:11**
>
> God worketh all things after the counsel of his own will.

This means God has a purpose and He works all situations out according to the counsel of His will. When you notice the move of the Holy Spirit in your life, it is to achieve God's purpose. God has a purpose for your journey to the next level and it is your responsibility to find it out.

> **PSALM 119:89**
>
> For ever, O Lord, thy word is settled in heaven.

If the word of God is settled forever, it indicates that God will not be ready for compromise. His word is solid and non-negotiable. So, no other foundation can be laid again apart from the one already laid by God. Therefore all creation must respond to God's word. Intimacy and frequent interaction with God give understand about His purpose for one's life. So before you begin a journey, you need to seek for God's opinion in order to know if it is in agreement with His purpose. There are blessings God has ordained for every stage of your life and God is ready to guide you in order to bring them into fulfilment. When you notice consistent failure of your visions, it is very likely you are not working in God's purpose. When you have to fold up projects due to lack of resources, it maybe that your purpose isn't of God. God will always make provisions for His visions.

Be Teachable

This requires the ability to accept and follow instructions.

> **PSALM 32:8**
>
> I will instruct thee and teach thee in the way which thou shalt go: I will guide thee with mine eye.

That is, God is ready to instruct and direct your journey. How will God teach you when you are not teachable? God operates through human vessels and He uses man to lift and direct another man. God operates through various means to pass messages across. If you don't regard men around you, how will God speak to you through them? Unfortunately, you will not be able to dictate to God whom He should send message through, to reach you. God can pass a message across to you even using the person you never imagined. There are road signs to follow in your journey to the next level and you must be ready to receive teaching for their meanings and interpretations. Spiritual facts are usually coded in spiritual language and teaching is required for understanding. Therefore, if you discover that you are always having breakdown and casualty in your journey to the next level, it may be because you have been ignoring God's warning.

Acknowledge God

> **PROVERB 3:5-7**
>
> Trust in the Lord with all thine heart; and lean not unto thine own understanding. In all thy ways acknowledge him, and he shall direct thy paths. Be not wise in thine own eyes: fear the Lord, and depart from evil.

For God to guide you through your journey, you must acknowledge Him. That is, you must admit and recognise that your success of reaching the next level is in God's hand. This is proved by seeking God in every stage of your journey. Therefore, you need to relinquish reliance on your own understanding and begin to trust God's ability to make a straight and profitable path for you. You need to humbly recognise God as the only One that can best control the affairs of your life. *2 Samuel 22:28* states that God will save the humble people. This is because the humble people will always accept instructions, so they are easy to guide. God made the way of David perfect (*2 Samuel 22:23*) because he always consulted God before he took any step irrespective of the urgency of the situation. David was never in a hurry as to forget consulting God in all his ways. God honours those that honour Him. Hence, if you have been experiencing aborted hope, it maybe because you are relying on your own limited understanding.

Trust God

God will only guide you when you trust him for guidance. Your faith has to please Him for Him to guide you through.

> **HEBREWS 11:6**
>
> But without faith it is impossible to please him: for he that cometh to God must believe that he is, and that he is a rewarder of them that diligently seek him.

God can't guide you when your faith displeases him. Faith will make you to be free from fear. Fear is of unbelief. When you dwell in fear, God is unable to guide you. Faith will make you to see God as able helper. Unbelief causes hesitation and prevents you from making exploit for God.

You should know that Jesus has destroyed the power of death and has released you from every manner of satanic bondage. Take hold of the freedom Jesus has granted you.

> **1 JOHN 4:4**
>
> Greater is he that is in you, than he that is in the world.

God who is guiding you is far greater than any obstacle on your journey. Your journey to the next level may require passing through difficult challenges but be assured that God is able to guide you through. Let faith produces patient in you. Give God the chance and time to guide you accordingly. Cast all your burdens onto Jesus. (*1 Peter 5:7*) Don't let unbelief distract you from your focus. Faith will also make you to avoid sins.

Be Separate

> **2 CORINTHIANS 6:17**
>
> Wherefore come out from among them, and be ye separate, saith the Lord, and touch not the unclean thing; and I will receive you.

For God to guide you on your journey, you need to come out of evil association. The people you hang around with will determine the chance of you receiving God's guidance. Evil association generates evil allies and influence that will close the door against God's guidance for your life. These are the people that pull you down. The Journey to the next level maybe lonely but get ready for it. To be successful on your journey, surround yourself with like minded people. There are many successful people in God's kingdom that you can associate with. They will motivate you. They will encourage you and create the conducive atmosphere for success around you. This permits the move of the Holy Spirit in your life. The calibre of people that surrounded David contributed immensely to his success both as a deliverer and the King of Israel (*1 Chronicle 12*).

PRAYER

Father, order my steps according to your purpose in Jesus name.

All evil collaborations arranged around my life by forces of hell, be scattered today in Jesus name. Father, let your light shine on my ways in Jesus name.

Every gap between me and my success, I close it by the fire of the Holy Ghost in Jesus name.

Every veil covering my understanding, be broken today in Jesus' name. Father grant me a teachable heart in Jesus name.

Father, advertise your favour in my life in Jesus name. The Lord Jesus, remove evil counsellor from my life in Jesus name.

Father, by your power, calm every storm rising against my purpose in Jesus name. The Lord Jesus, strengthen my faith to please God.

CHAPTER 4

HOLES IN THE ARMOUR

> **EPHESIANS 6:11**
>
> Put on the whole armour of God, that ye may be able to stand against the wiles of the devil.

An armour is a battle-dress worn by the first century Roman soldier. It is trusted for protection in battle. We are encouraged to put on the whole armour of God. This suggests that children of God are soldiers of Christ constantly at war against forces of evil. The journey to the next level will face opposition from the forces of evil, operating through human agents. The Devil will not fold his hands watching you rising from level to level. Therefore, you should dress for battle. You should be ready to stand against any opposition to your journey. Get ready to engage yourself in combat against the forces of evil. If your journey is of God, it will attract opposition from the kingdom of darkness. This is to prove it's genuineness and originality. The enemy's attack on God's purpose confirms that it is of God. The Devil will not oppose his own plan.

Darkness does not rise against darkness but against light. The good news is that the Devil has never won any battle against the children of God. Though the battle is certain, the victory is guaranteed through the power in the blood of Jesus (*Colossians 2:15*).

THE CHALLENGER

> **1 SAMUEL 17:4-10**
>
> And there went out a champion out of the camp of the Philistines, named Goliath, of Gath, whose height was six cubits and a span. And he had an helmet of brass upon his head, and he was armed with a coat of mail; and the weight of the coat was five thousand shekels of brass. And he had greaves of brass upon his legs, and a target of brass between his shoulders. And the staff of his spear was like a weaver's beam; and his spear's head weighed six hundred shekels of iron: and one bearing a shield went before him.
>
> And he stood and cried unto the armies of Israel, and said unto them, Why are ye come out to set your battle in array? am not I a Philistine, and ye servants to Saul? choose you a man for you, and let him come down to me. If he be able to fight with me, and to kill me, then will we be your servants: but if I prevail against him, and kill him, then shall ye be our servants, and serve us. And the Philistine said, I defy the armies of Israel this day; give me a man, that we may fight together.

The above verses suggest that:

1. Enemy is a challenger. Goliath challenges the Israelites for battle of supremacy. Up till today, the Devil is still operating through human agents to challenge the children of God. You don't need to commit any sin before the enemy challenges you. Darkness naturally hates light and forever darkness will continue to be an enemy of the light. Your success will liberate many other people from poverty and enslavement. The devil is fully aware that the consequence of your success will set some people free from the bondage he has put them for years. Therefore, he will make attempts to stop your journey to progress. So, whenever the devil rises against you, it is not only because of you but also because of those people your success may liberate in the future. The devil is a challenger, he challenges the children of God.

2. Enemy always dresses for battle. Goliath put on his own armour for battle against the Israelites. The armour of the enemy is always physical. That is why it is defeatable. His dressing was to intimidate people and instil fear in their minds. Unfortunately, many Christians succumb to the intimidation of the enemy. Enemy's weapons are canal, but ours are not canal but are mighty in God (2 *Corinthians 10:14*). He strategises, plans and organises his army for battle.

3. Enemy has a focus. Goliath declared that the winner would take all the victory, no sharing. That is, if you allow the devil to overpower your plan, expect total

occupation of your plan from him and soon he begins to expand his territory in your life.

He will begin to dictate the pace and take full control of your plan. It is, therefore, wise to resist him with all your strength. The devil always wants to rule over the children of God, so that he can exercise control over their destiny.

4. The enemy knows who you are. Demons recognise children of light. The devil is aware of your identity. He knows what you are up to when you set out. He knows you are destined for greatness. He knows the victory Jesus has won for you through the cross. The devil knows the truth though he rejects it, so, your journey to the next level isn't of secrecy. Therefore, be conscious of the devil's scheme and wile. Don't be ignorant of his devices.

HOLES IN THE ARMOUR

1 SAMUEL 18:49-50

And David put his hand in his bag, and took thence a stone, and slang it, and smote the Philistine in his forehead, that the stone sunk into his forehead; and he fell upon his face to the earth.

So David prevailed over the Philistine with a sling and with a stone, and smote the Philistine, and slew him; but there was no sword in the hand of David.

With all the dressing of Goliath, there was a hole in his armour. The stone of David was able to locate an opening within the forehead of Goliath. The devil is never perfect in his operation; always committing error. Similarly, many Christians leave holes in their armour. Ephesians 6:11 states that we should put on the whole armour. If there is a hole in your armour, you will be vulnerable to the enemy's attack. Many Christians win the victory but with casualty because there were holes in their armour. Many Christians live a life of defeat because they have created holes in their armour and this enable the arrow of the enemy to penetrate into their lives.

HOW DO YOU CREATE HOLES IN YOUR ARMOUR?

EPHESIANS 6:13-18

Wherefore take unto you the whole armour of God, that ye may be able to withstand in the evil day, and having done all, to stand. Stand therefore, having your loins girt about with truth, and having on the breastplate of righteousness; And your feet shod with the preparation of the gospel of peace; Above all, taking the shield of faith, wherewith ye shall be able to quench all the fiery darts of the wicked.

And take the helmet of salvation, and the sword of the Spirit, which is the word of God: Praying always with all prayer and supplication in the Spirit, and watching thereunto with all perseverance and supplication for all saints;

The above verses indicate that our warfare is not against people or any physical forces but against invisible powers who have clearly defined level of authority through invisible sphere of activity. These forces of hell however operate through human agents. To prevail against them, you need to put on the full armour of God and be on the offensive side, not defensive. The absence of any part of the amour creates holes on the armour and makes the person vulnerable.

LET US EXAMINE SOME OF THE ARMOUR

Belt of Truth

The belt holds the armour together and it is attached to the waist. The waist signifies the loin area. This represents part of you that is unseen. *Psalm 51:6* says God desires truth in the inward parts. Jesus is the truth *(John 14:6)*. Truth does not change and it does not have different version. Therefore, to put on the belt of truth means you walk and live as Jesus did *(1 John 17)*. There should be no lie within you. You must be real and genuine. You must walk in integrity and sincerity. Truth dispels darkness because it is light. Truth brings salvation *(2 Thessalonians 2:10)*. You can't prevail against the forces of hell when you display their attributes.

> **JOHN 8:44**
>
> Ye are of your father the devil, and the lusts of your father ye will do. He was a murderer from the beginning, and abode not in the truth, because there is no truth in him. When he speaketh a lie, he speaketh of his own: for he is a liar, and the father of it.

The above indicates that the devil abides not in the truth. No liar ever prevailed against the devil. Therefore, in your journey to the next level, ensure that no lie is found in you so that you can prevail against the devil and other forces of hell. Lie will create a big hole in your armour and will allow the enemy's arrow to penetrate. The word of God is the truth and whatever it says about every situation is the truth. Truth is different from the fact. The devil likes talking about fact and ignores the truth. You must always embrace the truth not the fact. For example it could be a fact that your sickness is incurable but the truth is that the word of God says that by the stripes of Christ you were healed (*1 Peter 2:24*). Similarly the word of God says in *Exodus 15:26* that it is the Lord that Healeth thee. That is, it is not man that will heal you but God. So, if man says he can't heal you, it does not mean you have reached the end of the road. Your healing is not from man but God.

Furthermore, the word of God says in *Psalm 118:17* that you shall not die but live. So if man says you will die, you should ignore because the God that has the final says about your case has said that you will live. If you ignore the truth and embrace the fact you will create a big hole in your armour. You must embrace and accept the report of God about every situation of your life. That is the truth. It may be a fact that you lack all resources to complete your dream but the word of God says in *Philippians 1:6* that God that started a good thing in your life shall complete it. Believe the truth and ignore the fact.

Breastplate of Righteousness

A soldier will put on breastplate to protect his heart against the enemy's arrow. The heart is the origin of desires and motivations. This indirectly dictates our actions. The heart filled with envy will generate vision and ambitions that originate from envy not the Spirit of God. Such plans will not receive God's provision and support. If your vision collapses you need to investigate it's origin whether it came from God or the flesh. Righteousness is based on your obedience to God.

> **ISAIAH 59:16-17**
>
> And he saw that there was no man, and wondered that there was no intercessor: therefore his arm brought salvation unto him; and his righteousness, it sustained him.
>
> For he put on righteousness as a breastplate, and an helmet of salvation upon his head; and he put on the garments of vengeance for clothing, and was clad with zeal as a cloke.

The above indicates the messiah dressing like a soldier to deal with his enemies. It affirms the victory that can be worn by a soldier that put on protective armour in the battle.

In *Joshua 7:5-11*, the Israelites couldn't prevail against their enemies; though they had strong fighting men of valour but unfortunately, they didn't put on the breastplate of righteousness. There was a hole in their armour, so they lost the battle. The problem was disobedience that crept into the camp through Achan-sin. The strongest man among the children of God wouldn't be able to prevail against the smallest demon in the absence of obedience to God.

Psalm 97:10 states that God delivers those that hate evil. There is victory and success in hating evil and clinging to righteousness. A man of upright heart will always prevail against forces of evil. *1 Kings 3:9* shows the prayer of Solomon for a discerning heart to enable him distinguish between right and wrong. Without this, there will be a big hole in the armour and the person becomes vulnerable .Therefore, if you constantly experience defeat without any sign of recovery, you need to investigate your heart and see whether it is constantly tuned to God or not.

Shoes of the Gospel

EPHESIANS 6:15

And your feet shod with the preparation of the gospel of peace.

The above indicates the importance of identifying yourself with God's kingdom. It is important that your life shows where you belong. Shoes enable smooth movement. They protect the feet and enable it to grip to the ground well. It prevents slipping. For you to be able to stand well against forces of hell, you need to put on shoes of the gospel of Jesus Christ. Without it, you will become easy prey for the enemy. The devil hates and fears testifiers. Your life must be a testimony. You must have something to share with others concerning your faith. Your lifestyle must also witness to people indirectly, that you are destroying the work of the devil.

> **ROMANS 1:16**
>
> For I am not ashamed of the gospel of Christ: for it is the power of God unto salvation to every one that believeth; to the Jew first, and also to the Greek.

The above verse reveals that there is an empowerment through support for the gospel of Jesus. God will always empower his instrument. In your journey to the next level, ensure that you cling to the business of the kingdom; be a testifier, seek for souls, enrich the souls of others and support the gospel. This is the key to victory over forces of hell. *Revelation 12:11* states that they overcame Satan by the blood of the lamb and by the word of their testimony. God is looking for a testifier to promote. A testifier makes God's work known to people. As you want God to be totally supportive in the fulfilment of your vision and dream, ensure that you also show your total support for God's work. Don't be selfish.

Shield of Faith

> **EPHESIANS 6:16**
>
> Above all, taking the shield of faith, wherewith ye shall be able to quench all the fiery darts of the wicked.

The above describes faith as a shield. That is, faith protects. It protects the mind, spirit and soul against the flaming arrows of the enemy. Such arrows include, discouragement, fear, anxiety, evil imagination, worry, emotional imbalance, unbelief etc. these are sent to destroy your faith. Faith for daily living is needed for victory over forces of evil.

> **1 JOHN 5:45**
>
> For whatsoever is born of God overcometh the world: and this is the victory that overcometh the world, even our faith. Who is he that overcometh the world, but he that believeth that Jesus is the Son of God?

Your faith in Christ overcomes the world. This is for defence. The book of *Hosea 4:6* says people are destroyed for lack of knowledge. It is also stated that faith comes by hearing, and hearing the word of God (*Romans 10:17*).

In a nutshell, your faith is enhanced by the level of knowledge you have regarding God's position concerning your plan. In the beginning of your journey, if you have received adequate information from God, it will enable you to stand against the lies of the enemy. Therefore, you need to arm yourself with the will of God concerning your plan and then stand on it. This dispels any arrow the enemy may fire at you. The revelation you have concerning your plan builds up unshakable confidence in you and you will be able to stand against enemy's manipulation. Hence, if you are thinking of abandoning your vision, it may be that you have not received enough revelation from God. When you are not sure of God's will concerning your plan, you will not be confident to resist the devil because you have no revelation to stand on. Therefore, it is important that before you begin your journey to the next level, you should seek God's face and equip yourself with revelation. Without these you have a big hole in your armour and when the enemy lies to you .You will not be able to resist him.

Helmet of Salvation

> **EPHESIANS 6:17**
>
> And take the helmet of salvation, and the sword of the Spirit, which is the word of God.

The helmet is put on the head. This is to protect the head, the seat of intelligence. This helps us to dispel the lies of the enemy. These lies may include false teaching that promotes self condemnation, creates guilty conscience, establishes inferiority complex and present God as a hater of men. It may affirm that your past sin is still active and that your present challenges are due to your sin. This is a game to weaken your morale. It is to breed within you that you can't prevail against the devil because you are a sinner and defenceless. Therefore ,you need to protect and shield your mind through the knowledge of salvation you have received from Christ.

> **1 THESSALONIANS 5:8**
>
> But let us, who are of the day, be sober, putting on the breastplate of faith and love; and for an helmet, the hope of salvation

The helmet, the hope of salvation. Your faith should be established in God's love.

> **ROMANS 8:1**
>
> There is therefore now no condemnation to them which are in Christ Jesus, who walk not after the flesh, but after the Spirit

The above indicates that you are free from God's judgement. The redemption work done by Christ is unchangeable. The Bible also states in Romans 8:38-39 that nothing can separate us from the love of God. Therefore never doubt your salvation irrespective of the situations around you. Even those who came before you faced challenges, so there is nothing unique about yours. Maintain your confidence and boldness in the face of any conflict. When you doubt God's love, you have created a big hole in your armour and the grace to win the battle may become weakened.

Sword of the Spirit

> **EPHESIANS 6:17**
>
> And take the helmet of salvation, and the sword of the Spirit, which is the word of God

The sword is the word of God. It is an offensive weapon. It is used to attack the enemy. The word of God may include the personal revelation you have received from God and also the word from the Bible. However, there is no personal revelation that is in contrary to the Bible. Every revelation from God agrees with the Bible.

> **PSALM 149:5-9**
>
> Let the saints be joyful in glory: let them sing aloud upon their beds.
>
> Let the high praises of God be in their mouth, and a two-edged sword in their hand;
>
> To execute vengeance upon the heathen, and punishments upon the people;
>
> To bind their kings with chains, and their nobles with fetters of iron;
>
> To execute upon them the judgment written: this honour have all his saints. Praise ye the Lord.

The above declares the word of God as a two-edged sword; a weapon of warfare, used to execute the written judgement on the enemies. *Hebrews 4:12-13* says God's word is sharper that the double-edged sword with an extreme ability to cut through any situations. In *Luke 4*, Jesus prevailed against Satan quoting the word of God. The devil can't resist God's word. Remember that devil also quotes the Bible but in a perverted form. He quotes bible to derail people. Therefore, you must know the word of God without alteration. The word of God also helps you not to go astray or stumble. (*John 16:1*). It gives you focus on the will of God concerning the plan. The word of God, when it is continually released, positions the enemy for defeat. In your journey to the next level, face every opposition with the word of God, soon, it will crumble. When the enemy attacks and you have no reply, you have created holes in your armour. Don't face forces of hell with psychology, philosophy of men, theories, traditions and scientific evidence. The devil is the originator of argument. Use the word of God.

Prayer in Warfare

The role of prayer can't be underestimated. Without it, the armour is useless and ineffective. Never be too busy to pray. Prayer is the means by which you engage in the battle. It is the Holy Spirit assisted prayer - it is in agreement with the word of God. It includes confession, adoration, thanksgiving, petition, intercession and supplication. It should be done without ceasing (*1 Thessalonians 5:17*). Through prayer, further guidance is received from God and the enemy's weaknesses are revealed. Prayer orchestrates events that will give birth to your expected ends. It positions the enemy for defeat.

> **2 SAMUEL 15:31**
>
> And one told David, saying, Ahithophel is among the conspirators with Absalom. And David said, O Lord, I pray thee, turn the counsel of Ahithophel into foolishness.

The above is a simple prayer made by David during Absalom's treason against him. Immediately David made the above prayer situations around Ahithopel began to form a pattern that will bring into fulfilment the prayer of David. Ahithopel unknowingly started acting out situations that will bring David's desire into fulfilment. *2 Samuel 17:23* states how Ahithopel's counsel was frustrated and led him to the death. Prayer from a pure heart is highly effective. Prayer ranges from form to form.

It could be a prophetic utterance like that of Moses; simple and effective.

> **EXODUS 14:13**
>
> And Moses said unto the people, Fear ye not, stand still, and see the salvation of the Lord, which he will shew to you to day: for the Egyptians whom ye have seen to day, ye shall see them again no more for ever

As Moses said so it was. When you operate through decree, you will be able to make a declaration that comes to pass. This will be possible when you manifest the mind of Christ (*1 Corinthians 2:16*) which will enable you to operate in the will of God concerning every situation.

It could be an aggressive prayer. Prayer must move you before it can move mountain.

> **1 KING 18:41-44**
>
> And Elijah said unto Ahab, Get thee up, eat and drink; for there is a sound of abundance of rain.
>
> So Ahab went up to eat and to drink. And Elijah went up to the top of Carmel; and he cast himself down upon the earth, and put his face between his knees,

> And said to his servant, Go up now, look toward the sea. And he went up, and looked, and said, There is nothing. And he said, Go again seven times.
>
> And it came to pass at the seventh time, that he said, Behold, there ariseth a little cloud out of the sea, like a man's hand. And he said, Go up, say unto Ahab, Prepare thy chariot, and get thee down, that the rain stop thee not.

In the above paragraph, though Elijah had the promise of God concerning rain yet he prayed aggressively; and he never stopped praying until the rain fell. Never stop praying until your joy is full irrespective of the certainty of your hope. Your consistency in prayer reflects your faith in the answer.

Through prayer we receive strength to face the cross on our journey to the next level.

> **LUKE 22:41-44**
>
> And he was withdrawn from them about a stone's cast, and kneeled down, and prayed,
>
> Saying, Father, if thou be willing, remove this cup from me: nevertheless not my will, but thine, be done.

The Lord Jesus prayed aggressively and when the flesh wanted to manifest, the angels of God gave him strength. The strength to forge ahead to the next level is received during prayer. Effective prayer needs your motivation, full concentration, and involvement of your heart. The Lord Jesus prayed with his full strength. When you pray, never forget to still pray. This is because when your prayer hits the camp of the enemy repeatedly, he will react; but continuous prayer overcomes every manner of aggression from the enemy's camp. Some years ago, through the revelation from God, R.C.C.G in the Kingdom of Lesotho, Southern Africa was given an assignment to pray for the land of Lesotho. So, in obedience, we gathered ourselves together. The group involved interested ministers and parish pastors of R.C.C.G in the land. We went on an intense fasting and prayer. We were led by the Holy Spirit to gather relevant information concerning the country. This includes information concerning the origin of Christianity in the land, the founding fathers of the country and the culture and tradition of the people of the land. We were led to visit some strategic locations in the land that are of historic importance to the prayer and fasting and we equipped ourselves with the anointing oil to anoint some structures within the land and the assignment was completed after some weeks.

Few days after this, the forces of evil started operating through the government of the day with threat that the country did not need missionaries and that some foreign indigenes such as Nigerians must leave the country. It was clear that the enemy was reacting to the just concluded assignment God had given us. We continued to pray and pray until the threat was dissolved and blown away. Therefore, be vigilant on your way to the next level. Keep on praying and never allow increase in challenges to force you out of the way. It is an indication that your prayer is effective.

PRAYER

Father, paralyse my oppressor in Jesus name.

Father, position my enemy for defeat in Jesus name.

Father, the mistake my enemy will make that will advance my destiny, ordain it by your power in Jesus name.

Father, every hole in my armour, seal it up with the blood of Jesus.

I loose my self from every manner of demonic control in Jesus name.

Every cloud of darkness covering my potentials, be broken today in Jesus name.

The Lord Jesus protect my vision from the secret plot of the enemy.

Every ground I have lost to the enemy, I regain it today in Jesus name.

Father, mark my effort for success in Jesus name.

Father, arise and scatter all enemies of my salvation in Jesus name.

CHAPTER 5

JOURNEY IN STAGES

Your journey to the next level will take place in stages. God will move you from stage to stage until you reach your destination. Perhaps, you desire to move to the next level in your ministry, business, career, education or profession, you need to understand that it will be accomplished in stages.

Why should your journey be in stages? *Romans 8:29* states that for whom God foreknew he also predestined to be confirmed to the image of his son. This implies that all that God will allow you to face in life is to make you to be like Jesus. Therefore, God allows and designs it such that your path to greatness will not be all smooth so that you will develop a new nature that will conform to that of Jesus. Hence, there will be a sequel of events that will unfold themselves stage by stage until you complete the journey. It is through this journey that we develop spiritual muscles. Those challenges are the ones that build up our faith in the deliverance power of God.

THE BLUEPRINT OF THE JOURNEY

2 KINGS 2:1-9

And it came to pass, when the Lord would take up Elijah into heaven by a whirlwind, that Elijah went with Elisha from Gilgal.

And Elijah said unto Elisha, Tarry here, I pray thee; for the Lord hath sent me to Bethel. And Elisha said unto him, As the Lord liveth, and as thy soul liveth, I will not leave thee. So they went down to Bethel.

And the sons of the prophets that were at Bethel came forth to Elisha, and said unto him, Knowest thou that the Lord will take away thy master from thy head to day? And he said, Yea, I know it; hold ye your peace.

And Elijah said unto him, Elisha, tarry here, I pray thee; for the Lord hath sent me to Jericho. And he said, As the Lord liveth, and as thy soul liveth, I will not leave thee. So they came to Jericho.

And the sons of the prophets that were at Jericho came to Elisha, and said unto him, Knowest thou that the Lord will take away thy master from thy head to day? And he answered, Yea, I know it; hold ye your peace.

And Elijah said unto him, Tarry, I pray thee, here; for the Lord hath sent me to Jordan. And he said, As the Lord liveth, and as thy soul liveth, I will not leave thee. And they two went on.

And fifty men of the sons of the prophets went, and stood to view afar off: and they two stood by Jordan.

> And Elijah took his mantle, and wrapped it together, and smote the waters, and they were divided hither and thither, so that they two went over on dry ground.
>
> And it came to pass, when they were gone over, that Elijah said unto Elisha, Ask what I shall do for thee, before I be taken away from thee. And Elisha said, I pray thee, let a double portion of thy spirit be upon me.

The above details the story of the journey of Elisha to the next level. He desires to have a double portion of the anointing that was upon Elijah, his master. This vision took him through four different locations on his journey to the next level which includes: Gilgal to Bethel to Jericho to Jordan. These four locations have spiritual meaning to every Christian that desires to move to the next level. The understanding of the relevance will revolutionize your attitude towards life ambition. To give a clearer understanding of its meaning, the life of David shall be used as a case study. This will enable you to fix your situation into the whole episode and assist you to be wiser than your enemy.

CASE STUDY

Let us learn how David passed through the journey on his way to rule the Israelites.

Gilgal Experience

The journey to the next level begins in Gilgal. What does Gilgal represent?

> **JOSHUA 5:8-9**
>
> And it came to pass, when they had done circumcising all the people, that they abode in their places in the camp, till they were whole.
>
> And the Lord said unto Joshua, This day have I rolled away the reproach of Egypt from off you. Wherefore the name of the place is called Gilgal unto this day.

The above shows the circumcision of the Israelites for the second time. The older generation that were circumcised had died apart from people like Joshua and Caleb. The older generation died during the 40 years of wilderness experience due to their sin *(Numbers 14:26-34)*. That is, before they reached Gilgal the camp was made up of the circumcised and uncircumcised. Spiritually the circumcised represent the group of people with faith (spirit) while the uncircumcised were people without faith, that is, unbelief (the flesh). Hence, the group before Gilgal was made up of a mixture of faith and unbelief.

That is at Gilgal:

1. God put an end to a little bit of faith and a little bit of unbelief. Double nature ends at Gilgal. God get rid of doubt.

2. God rolls away the reproach of Egypt *(Joshua 5:9)*. That is all the ties they had with Egyptian enslavery ended at Gilgal. That implies that products of enslavement such as frustration, bondage, sin, futile effort, perversion of destiny etc were cut off from the Israelites.

3. God arranged spiritual cleansing for His people. All spiritual pollution ended at Gilgal.

David had Gilgal experience for God to notice his qualification to be king.

> **1 SAMUEL 13:14**
>
> But now thy kingdom shall not continue: the Lord hath sought him a man after his own heart, and the Lord hath commanded him to be captain over his people, because thou hast not kept that which the Lord commanded thee.

God declares that David is a man after his own heart. That is, David was a man of circumcised heart. It was the nature of David's heart that attracted God's attention to David.

Colossians 2:11 states that there is a circumcision done without hand or knife but by the Holy Spirit. This implies that David had allowed his heart to be circumcised by the Holy Spirit even before God picked him up. God pick up David and anointed him in *1 Samuel 16:13* and power came upon him. With a circumcised heart and anointing of God upon David, he became undefeatable. No wonder he outlived his enemies.

Consequences of the anointing on David are many and they include:

1. David was taken out of obscurity to light. (*1 Samuel 16:18*). The world began to notice David's potential. All the ties David had with obscurity were broken.

2. David started having audience with the king (*1 Samuel 16:21*). He became the king's helper. The situation that would make the king to seek David's help began to arise.

3. David received empowerment. He needed strength of the spirit to complete his journey to the next level.

If you want to complete your journey to the next level, you need the Gilgal experience. Your heart needs to be circumcised. When you meet this condition, the anointing of the Holy Ghost comes upon you on its own accord. David didn't seek Samuel to anoint him. It was God that orchestrated it because he had an upright heart. Even if you manipulate your way through for man to anoint you with oil, it will be ineffective because a circumcised heart needs to be present for the anointing to give empowerment. A man of circumcised heart finds it easy to trust God to complete what he started in his life. With the anointing of God coming upon you, you will not find it difficult to fight battles. Anointing terminates frustration and other products of enslavement. An anointed person can't be hidden for long; the anointing upon him will bring him out of obscurity.

Bethel Experience

The next stage of your journey to the next level will be Bethel.

What does Bethel represent?

According to *Genesis 28:17-49* Bethel means 'the House of God'. The House of God is a place of grace. Grace is the free mercy of God or the enjoyment of his favour. What are the importance of this in your journey?

1. The grace enables you to conquer your strong enemies and win your battles on the way to the next level. The grace enables you to come out victoriously when you face the battles you can't fight by yourself.

2. The grace positions you for success and your enemy for failure. David had a Bethel experience on his way to possessing his possession.

> **1 SAMUEL 17:40**
>
> And he took his staff in his hand, and chose him five smooth stones out of the brook, and put them in a shepherd's bag which he had, even in a scrip; and his sling was in his hand: and he drew near to the Philistine

David took five stones on his way to fight Goliath. The Spiritual meaning of five is grace. It was God's grace that gave him victory over Goliath not the effectiveness of the stones. Grace makes success to be easily achievable. The battle that people with the sophisticated weapon could not win David won it with ordinary stone. That was grace at work.

In *1 Samuel 18:7*, the world began to celebrate David. David had made success that would advertise him to the bigger world. Note that at Gilgal experience, David was advertised to King Saul, but here at Bethel experience God begins to advertise David to the whole world. God is promoting him little by little. It is a journey, he is going somewhere.

If you want to complete your journey, you need the grace of God. It is this grace that gives sustenance. Whatever the challenge on your way, remember that God's grace is always available to record victory.

As the battle rages on, so God releases more grace on you. This is the reason why you should not fear any battle and also recognise that it is the Lord's grace that will give you victory not your ability or strength. If God is involved in your journey there will always be grace to sustain you and help you not to give up.

2 Corinthians 12:9 states that God's grace is sufficient. This is what guarantees victory in any battle. The level you are now was made possible through the grace of God and it is the same grace that will take you to the next level.

Jericho Experience

Welcome to Jericho.

What does Jericho represent?

> **JOSHUA 6:1**
>
> Now Jericho was straitly shut up because of the children of Israel: none went out, and none came in.

Jericho was a city surrounded with strong walls. This was to prevent the Israelites from having access unto their inheritance. These walls can't be brought down by human efforts. So in *Joshua 6:2*, God told Israelites not to use their own effort to bring down the walls. So, in this context,

Jericho represents an obstacle that you can't handle by your effort. Therefore, you must recognise the boundaries of your mandate given to you by God. There are battles your anointing can't handle.

David had the Jericho experience.

> **1 SAMUEL 20:31**
>
> For as long as the son of Jesse liveth upon the ground, thou shalt not be established, nor thy kingdom. Wherefore now send and fetch him unto me, for he shall surely die.

The above reflects that Saul was fully aware that David was a future king. As long as Saul was alive, David could never rule Israel as king. So, Saul had to die for David to rule. To worsen the matter, David had no mandate to kill Saul with his own hands.

Twice, (1 Samuel 24:6,26:9-10) David had opportunities to kill Saul but he didn't. What a wall! This was a wall separating David from his inheritance and yet he could not raise his hands against him. Worst still, Saul was always ready to eliminate David. The grace of God that enabled David to record victory over Goliath who he fought with his hand also protected him from the hands of Saul that he could not fight. In 1 Samuel 27:1 David became hopeless and he became a wandering star. Jericho is a place of hopelessness; but victory will come at last. So, what appears like a wall before you? Are you passing through some bitter experiences? Are you facing a hopeless situation? Though you have heard from God before you launched out but the situations don't portray that God is involved. Perhaps you are thinking of quitting the journey? Maybe you are facing a situation that appears like Saul, deadly, yet you can't rise against it.

> **JOB 42:2**
>
> I know that thou canst do every thing, and that no thought can be withholden from thee

There is no force or counsel or wall that can abort God's purpose. The end of every battle has been declared before it came to existence. Though you may not see it, God has put the natural systems that will swallow every Saul in your life at the appointed time. When the time comes, your Saul shall be no more because the systems God has put in position will always out live the enemies. Are you facing a wall? Start praising God concerning it. Soon, it will crumble. Don't quit your journey to the next level because of strong opposition. Press on. You will seek your enemies but they shall be no more. (*Isaiah 41:12*). Whatever is separating you from your inheritance shall give way. Whoever the devil is using to pursue or frustrate your journey shall not succeed. *Job 5:12* declares that God frustrates the devices of the crafty so that their hands can't carry out their plans. You will soon testify to this statement. The triumph of the wicked is for a short time. Whatever situation that seems unconquerable before you will soon be no more. Your Saul is on his way to his grave. So, get ready for a surprise. Though, it may appear as if the enemy is winning, don't be carried away, he is moving and dancing towards his grave! (*Job 20:5*).

The purpose of God will always be tested and the man of destiny will be allowed to face opposition. The bigger the destiny, the bigger the opposition. The intention is to build him up and to produce a total man. Unless gold passes through fire, it shall never shine.

Jordan Experience

What does Jordan represent?

Jordan could be described as:

1. A place of transformation. *Joshua 3:15-16* indicates that the Israelites crossed over River Jordan.

> **JOSHUA 4:23**
>
> For the Lord your God dried up the waters of Jordan from before you, until ye were passed over, as the Lord your God did to the Red sea, which he dried up from before us, until we were gone over

   Jordan is a place of crossing over; crossing over from the old to a new life. A place of rebirth. At Jordan, all impossibilities end. It is a new life; a life of possibilities.

2. A place of divine exaltation.

   God exalted Joshua at Jordan, *Joshua 3:7, 4:14*. Elisha was exalted at Jordan, *1 Kings 2:6, 13*. The Lord Jesus was exalted at Jordan, *Matthew 3:13-17*. This is a place of elevation before the whole world.

3. A place of open heaven. Heaven opened over Jesus at Jordan, *Matthew 3:16*. From here Jesus entered into His ministry fully with the power of the Holy Ghost.

David also passed through the Jordan experience. Suddenly Saul died, (*1 Samuel 31:3*) without David's involvement. Heavens opened over his life. Hopeless situations changed. People came to David on their own accord to make him king (*2 Samuel 2:4; 5:1-3*).

God exalted David to the throne of honour. Walls collapsed on their own accord.

In *Psalm 75:6-7*, the king went into retrospect. He considered all he had passed through. He looked into the beginning when he was anointed to be king and yet he didn't come to the throne. He considered how he killed mighty Goliath with ordinary stone. He considered his days as a shepherd. He looked into how far God had led him. David was convinced it had been God, not men. To David, it was God that pulled down Saul to exalt him. As you are reading this book, you are crossing over from impossibility to possibility, failure to success, rejection to approval and stagnancy to advancement. Henceforth, heavens begin to recommend you for a position of honour. The realm of the divine supernatural will give final approval concerning your promotion, healing, break-through and miracles. Whatever needs to be pulled down for you to be exalted shall be pulled down by God today in Jesus name.

Finally, know this...

The journey to the next level is:

1. Initiated by God

2. Your role is to respond to the touch of God concerning the vision and dream he Has been dropping into your spirit.

3. It is completed by the Spirit of God, not by the power of men, *Zechariah 4:6*. If God started it, He will complete it, *Philippians 1:6*.

Your journey will take you through Gilgal, Bethel, Jericho and Jordan. Whatever stage you are now, remember God is the one that will carry you through it. (*Isaiah 46:4*)

PRAYER

Father, I thank You for You are always carrying me in Your hands.

Father, I thank you because I am never alone, for your presence is always with me.

The Lord Jesus, the grace that will grant me victory over all challenges of my life, release on me today.

The Lord Jesus, keep me away from temptation of revenge.

Father, whatever is in me that is capable of frustrating my vision, take it out by your power in Jesus name.

Father, you are a God that rules over season, take me into the season of fulfilment by your power in Jesus name.

Father, by your power, frustrate every counsel of hosts of hell concerning my destiny.

Father, protect me from the attack of envious people.

Every regime of oppression set over my life, Father dethrone them today in Jesus name.

The Lord Jesus, turn my battle ground to a place of worship for me.

CHAPTER 6

STRENGTH FOR THE JOURNEY

Strength is the ability to complete a task. The Journey to the next level will require strength. You need to display enough strength for you to reach the next level. Strength will take you from stage to stage until you get to the height you desire. The kind of strength you will need is beyond the natural because some of the hindrances you will face on the journey have spiritual connections. You will need to go beyond human ability if you want to successfully reach the next level in any area of your life. Therefore, you will need divine strength.

> **ISAIAH 40:31**
>
> But they that wait upon the Lord shall renew their strength; they shall mount up with wings as eagles; they shall run, and not be weary; and they shall walk, and not faint.

The above Bible verse gives an indication of the kind of strength you will need in order to reach the next level.

You will need the strength of an eagle. Eagles display the nature of strength God wants to give you so as to reach the next level. Therefore, studying the eagles will enlighten you about how to develop the kind of strength you need for the journey to the next level.

Eagles are wonderful birds with attributes that will take anybody to the next level in any area of his or her life. Let us study Eagles and learn how to develop the strength that will take us to the next level.

1. EAGLES ASCEND

Eagles can fly well over thousands of altitude at a high speed within a short time. According to *Isaiah 40:31*, you are supposed to mount up wings like eagles so as to be able to fly higher in life. Eagles are able to ascend because they have enough ability to fight the wind resistance that may want to oppose their movements. For you not to stay too long in one place, you will need to get ready to fight your way to the next level. Rising needs fighting. There is a gravity that always attempts to stop people from rising. There is a gravity that will attempt to pull you down as you attempt to rise but you must be ready to fight them and never surrender to their dictate. There is gravity everywhere in life. There is gravity at a place of work that may want to oppose your promotion. There could be gravity at the marital home that wants to press you down and frustrate you out of your marriage. There could be gravity in your company that want to frustrate all your effort for increased sales. In *1 Samuel 17:28*, Eliab, the brother of David showed up as a gravity to shout down David but David resisted him. After that event David rose up in life. Be ready to fight any gravity that wants to oppose your journey to the next level. Don't surrender but resist. I pray that the Lord will strengthen you to rise above every gravity that wants to press you down in Jesus name.

2. EAGLES RUN WITHOUT BEING WEARY

The Bible verse of *Isaiah 40:31*, states that eagles don't get weary. The question is: what makes eagles to be able to run without being weary? It is because eagles run effortlessly. When the storm comes, the eagle spreads its wings and never flutter them. Eagles don't move their wings while inside the storm; but just spread them out. That is, the storm carries the eagles forward. Eagles ride on the wind.

> **PSALMS 104:3**
>
> Who layeth the beams of his chambers in the waters: who maketh the clouds his chariot: who walketh upon the wings of the wind.

The above verse states that the Lord walks on the wings of the wind. Do you know that most of the great plans of God for your life will be achieved through the storm and challenges of your life? God will allow storm and challenges to come on your way and he will use them as vehicles to carry his divine plans into manifestation in your life. God uses your struggles to lead you into his plans for your life. It is the challenges of your life that God will mount on to take you to the next level.

For you not to miss out of the great plans of God for your life, you will need to behave like eagles. You need to run effortlessly. This is achieved by running, relying on God's strength and not yours.

Joseph in the Bible ran effortlessly. He stayed calm and waited on the Lord and soon, the storm of his life carried him to the position of the Prime-Minister in Egypt. Joseph spread out his wings while inside storms and never fluttered them. He remained calm inside all his challenges and soon, challenges disappeared on their own accord. Joseph never argued or fought anybody even when he was being lied against. He was calm and in control of his senses. He rested on the deliverance that would come from God and He reached the next level.

Don't waste time fighting those that are lying against you. Don't waste time to defend yourself before those that hate you for no reason. Don't allow the enemy to take control of your mind from you. Don't waste your energy by focusing on what the enemy is doing in your life. Keep your focus on the higher level you are going. When the enemy discover that you are too busy to give him attention, he will leave you alone. Eagles don't struggle with storm. Just remain calm and soon, you will see your storm carrying you to the next level.

3. EAGLES CAN SEE FAR

Eagle is able to spot a prey at a far distance and successfully dive at it.

> **JOB 39:27-29**
>
> Doth the eagle mount up at thy command, and make her nest on high? She dwelleth and abideth on the rock, upon the crag of the rock, and the strong place. From thence she seeketh the prey, and her eyes behold afar off.

The above verse shows that the eagle can see far. The eagle is able to prepare itself to catch an animal because it is able to see far.

The Journey to the next level will require that you are able to see far. Only those who are able to detect an opportunity at a distance can adequately prepare for it. Intuition is the ability to discern and identify opportunities. You will need to develop the power of an intuition in order to be able to see far in life and prepare for what is coming.

> **1 CORINTHIANS 2:15**
>
> But he that is spiritual judgeth all things, yet he himself is judged of no man.

The above Bible verse states that a spiritual man judges all things. That is, he is able to probe into the situation in order to see beyond it. He meditates, evaluates and thoroughly considers a situation. This gives him access into hidden details concerning the situation. There are signs that introduce every season before it is fully manifest. For examples, there are certain signs you will notice when winter or summer is about to fully come. Those that can interpret the signs will start preparing for the coming seasons. Such people will not be caught in the water of surprise when the seasons arrive. There are many signs that will come ahead of the situations of your life. God allows it, so that you can prepare for what is coming and take full advantage of it. At your place of work there could be some signs that will come to let you know that very soon there will be vacancies at the top. Once you notice this, you need to look inward and see if you will fit into those positions when they come. If you discover that you will not fit into it, then you need to start making yourself fit by attending to your weaknesses. Do you know that economic crisis in any nation brings opportunities to those that are able to see beyond the crisis?

The Journey to the next level will require that you open your inner eyes to see beyond the present so as to prepare for the future. As God is taking you higher, He will be opening some opportunities that will come in a subtle way. Only those with intuition will notice it afar and prepare for it. Through intuition, you will be able to always be ahead of your competitors in all situations. Give careful consideration to every situations that come on your ways because there will always be something good inside of it. May you always be ahead of your competitors in Jesus name.

4. EAGLES ARE ABLE TO CAPTURE WHAT THEY SEE

It is one thing to see opportunities at a distance and prepare for them; but it is another thing to be able to capture them as they arrive. For example in *Deuteronomy 34:1-4*, at Pisgah, Moses saw the Promised Land at a distance but never possessed it. The spirit of Pisgah would not let Moses possess the Promised Land. This could be described as the spirit of 'Almost-there'. This is a spirit that mounts on human weakness to rub him of the promises of God. Moses problem was his personal weakness that he never attended to. He would have dealt with anger before he reached the place of Pisgah. He had so many opportunities on the way to deal with his anger but he missed them. Moses prayed to God on many things but he never remembered to pray to God to help him overcome the spirit of anger.

The Journey to the next level will reveal your vulnerabilities as you progress. Challenges on the way will reveal what is inside of you that wants to frustrate your journey. These, you will need to quickly cut off from your life as they manifest. For example, if you discover that you find it difficult to let offence go without bitterness, it means you will need to deal with un-forgiveness. Also, if you notice that you unknowingly speak evil word when situations become rough, it means you will need to deal with your tongue. You may also notice as you progress in the journey that you always find it hard to locate important documents you once received from certain people. It means you need to deal with your management ability. Perhaps you notice that you always forget appointment, it means you need to pay attention to record keeping. If you always procrastinate in taking major actions, you will need to attend to time management. Similarly, you may notice in your life that plans always go wrong at the point of execution, it means you need to attend to the way you prepare for a task. As you progress in the journey of life, don't miss opportunities to attend to your personal weaknesses.

There are many people that will see opportunities at a distance but they fail at the stage of grabbing them. This is because their personal weaknesses override their efforts. Avoid blaming people and circumstances around you when situations go wrong. Always take responsibility for all that happens in your life. This will help you attend to your weaknesses and come out of them. It is my prayer that every veil preventing you from identifying your weaknesses shall be cut off from your life today in Jesus name.

5. EAGLES PROTECT THEIR VISIONS

Eagles have a clear and thick membrane that protects their sight. This protects their eyes from any danger when catching the prey. Protection needs strength because there are dangers around. You need to know how to protect your visions, dreams and plans because there are enemies that want to scatter them. Whatever is not protected is vulnerable to attack. The Journey to the next level will require that you protect your goals. In *Nehemiah 4:17-23*, those building with Nehemiah held weapons in one hand while using the second hand to work. They were protecting their task against enemy's attack. Protect your visions.

There are vision killers around. One of the ways to protect your vision is by controlling your tongue.

> **PROVERBS 21:23**
>
> Whoso keepeth his mouth and his tongue keepeth his soul from troubles.

If you can learn how to keep your mouth shut concerning what you are chasing, you will escape so many attacks in life. People that have no role to play in your journey don't need to know about it. People that God has not sent to build with you have no right to know all the details of what is going on in your life. In *Genesis 37*, Joseph invited avoidable attack into his life because he told his brothers his dreams. He told his dream to those that had no dream. When you share your dream with those that have no dream, you will provoke envy from them. You don't journey with those who are not going to the same destination with you. There are people that have no vision and if you should tell them your vision, they develop a vision on how to attack your vision. Some peoples' vision is how to destroy the visions of others. You will escape their evil if you learn how to keep your mouth shut. Seek wisdom on how to protect your vision and you will never fail.

In *Judges 16*, Samson failed to protect anointing of God upon his life by mingling with Delilah. He eventually lost his eyes and later died with his enemies. Avoid mingling with those that have no relationship with your God otherwise, they will become a channel of destruction to you. In *1 Samuel 30:1-25*. David failed to arrange protection for his home and enemies came behind him to take all he had away. Avoid being short-sighted. Develop an attitude that gives priority to security. Be conscious of vision killers because they exist. It is my prayer that every attack hell had organised against your life shall fail in Jesus name.

6. EAGLES ADD KNOWLEDGE TO PASSION

Eagles are passionate about dead animals to eat. Eagles can run after dead lion to eat but you will never see eagles running after a lion that is alive. The eagle knows and sees well its preys before diving towards them. On your journey to the next level you will need to add knowledge to passion. It is good to have passion to further your education but it is also good to have understanding of what is driving you and how you will achieve your purpose. You must know what you are doing and why you are doing what you are doing. There are things you need to do to get your dream and there are things you are not supposed to do in order to get your dream.

In *Leviticus 10:1*, the sons of Aaron had a passion to make sacrifices to the Lord but did not add knowledge to it and fire consumed them. They never found out about what must be done and what must not be done when making sacrifice to the Lord. Passion without knowledge will lead to avoidable destruction. It will also make you to carry loads which are beyond your capability. Some struggles are avoidable if there is enough knowledge. With knowledge, you can escape some challenges. With knowledge you can get to the next level without wearing yourself out. It is not only about how hard you work but also how smart you work. The Journey to the next level will expose you to series of temptations but it is the knowledge that will deliver you. With knowledge you can minimise or eliminate waste of resources. With knowledge you can discover an easy route to achieve your dream. Seek for relevant knowledge before you pursue your vision. Find out from those that have reached greater heights in the similar dream you are pursuing and learn from them. Don't just run but run with wisdom. It is my prayer that any area of your life that is engulfed in darkness shall receive the light of God today in Jesus name.

7. EAGLES ARE COURAGEOUS

Courage is strength. Eagles fly toward storm without fear. The eagle is not afraid of storm and that is why it is able to fly at the altitude other birds dare not fly due to fear of the storm. Courage could be defined as the ability to face difficult situation without distraction from a chosen course. A courageous person will press on with his dream even when he comes across challenges. He will refuse to quit. The Journey to the next level will require courage because there are challenges on the way that you will need to confront and overcome. In *Joshua 1:9*, God told Joshua to be strong and be of good courage. This is because there are challenges on the way, yet the mission must be accomplished. The journey must progress despite difficulties. You must show courage at the face of whatever the enemy is throwing on your way to stop you. You must press on and not quit. Refuse to bow to intimidation, harassment and any form of attack. Remember that a quitter never wins and a winner never quits. One of the outstanding blessings of courage is that it gives you grace under pressure. This grace enables you to treat things that exist as if they don't. It enables you to face danger as if there is no danger. For example, it was courage that made David (*I Samuel 17*) to face Goliath. Truly Goliath was taller and more experienced than David in battle but David ignored all these and treated them as if they did not exist. David did not see what advantage Goliath had over him when it came to battle. That is grace and it comes from courage. Similarly it was courage that made Caleb and Joshua to believe that the Amalekites could be defeated despite the fact that they were taller and huge (*Numbers 13:14*).

There are facts and there are truths. The facts are what your senses notice. Facts come from reality of life. It could be a fact that your opponents are better placed to defeat you due to their positive attributes that are visible. The truth comes from what the word of God says concerning the situations. For example *Philippians 4:13* says that you can do all things through Christ that strengthen you. That is, there is no battle you can't win with Christ giving you strength. This is the truth and it does not change. All the men of God that gained victory in the battles of life lived on truth not fact. This is the bedrock of their courage.

When you read in the Bible that Daniel was not moved when he was thrown into the den of lion, it was because he focused on the truth not fact. Lions can truly kill but there is a God that holds power over any lion; and that is the same God that was on the side of Daniel. Daniel focused on the God that can control lions instead of focusing on the lions. That is wisdom. It was the truth that made the disciples to rejoice when being thrown into prison. Those that threw them inside prison truly had evil intentions but disciples focused on God that rules in the affairs of men.

For Shadrach, Meshach, and Abednego to be unmoved when facing fire in *Daniel 3*, there must be something they focused on that is greater than fire. That is the truth. Fire can't kill the truth neither can it defeat it. Courage is greater than fire. Courage is greater than the kings and queens of the earth. There is no trouble you can't defeat with courage. There is no challenge you can't overthrow with courage. Learn how to focus on the God who is always on your side and you will see yourself rising above every storm. I pray that courage that can't be defeated by the enemy shall be established in your spirit today in Jesus name.

8. EAGLES SOAR

To soar means to increase quickly to a higher level. Eagles fly to a higher altitude within a short time. It is also possible for you to soar in your journey to the next level. It is possible for you to reach a higher level in your dream within a short time. It is very possible for your promotion to be fast forwarded. You can experience supernatural and accelerated promotion in your mission. The journey that was supposed to take you years can take you months. The strength to soar is available.

> **1 KINGS 18:42-46**
>
> So Ahab went up to eat and to drink. And Elijah went up to the top of Carmel; and he cast himself down upon the earth, and put his face between his knees, and said to his servant, Go up now, look toward the sea. And he went up, and looked, and said, There is nothing. And he said, Go again seven times. And it came to pass at the seventh time, that he said, Behold, there ariseth a little cloud out of the sea, like a man's hand. And he said, Go up, say unto Ahab, Prepare thy chariot, and get thee down, that the rain stop thee not. And it came to pass in the meanwhile, that the heaven was black with clouds and wind, and there was a great rain. And Ahab rode, and went to Jezreel. And the hand of the Lord was on Elijah; and he girded up his loins, and ran before Ahab to the entrance of Jezreel.

In the above story, Elijah soared in speed. He out-ran Ahab that was long gone. The journey that was supposed to take Elijah hours took him less time. What is the secret of Elijah's outstanding performance against King Ahab? The hand of God came upon Elijah to give him strength to run ahead of King Ahab. It is also stated in the story that Elijah went on fasting and intense prayer while King Ahab was busy eating and drinking. If you can do what your mates fail to do, you will see yourself go ahead of them in life. In your journey to the next level, if you can regularly set aside some days for fasting and intense prayer to God, you will provoke the hand of God to rest upon you for accelerated speed. It is possible to soar but it requires supernatural strength.

9. EAGLES HAVE DISTINCT ATTRACTION

Attraction is to be drawn towards a thing. There are things that attract eagles.

> **MATTHEW 24:28**
>
> For wheresoever the carcase is, there will the eagles be gathered together.

The above indicates that eagles are attracted towards carcase. It is not everything that attracts eagles. Eagles have taste.

In your journey to the next level you will be faced with different options and you will need to make choices. Your taste will determine your choices. Strength is needed to make the right choices. You need strength to resist things that appear good but not beneficial. In *Daniel 1*, Daniel chose not to eat royal food but preferred vegetables. He had enough strength to resist the delicacy of royal food. Daniel preferred to please God rather than his pleasures. His taste is different. If wrong things taste nice to you, there will be complication on the journey to the next level. In *Hebrew 11:24-25*, Moses chose to belong to the family of God because he wanted to please God. On your journey to the next level, you will face situations where you have to make a decision between pleasing God and yourself. You will always get things right if it is your habit to please God. In *1 King 3:9*, Solomon asked for wisdom to enable him to discern between good and evil. Sometime the line of demarcation between good and evil is very thin and wisdom is the only strength that can help to make correct choices. Do you have taste for pleasing God? If pleasing God attracts you always, you will always make right choices when faced with more than one option. Can you differentiate minor from major? In *Luke 10:41-42*, Martha focused on the minor (physical food) while Mary focused on the major (spiritual food). In your journey to the next level, you should be able to make a difference between minor and major. It is better to let major things attract you and let minor be minor. If you give too much attention to the minor things, your journey to the next level will suffer delay. Don't be carried away with petty things. Major on the major and be minor on the minor. Which kinds of people attract you? In *Ruth 1:16*, Naomi, a member of God's family, attracted Ruth. Ruth would not depart from Naomi. Her choice brought her into the household of God. If godly people attract you, you will always be in the company of good people. Do you have a taste for godly relationship? May God empower you for right attraction in Jesus name.

10. THE EAGLE SEPARATES ITSELF

JOB 39:27-28

Doth the eagle mount up at thy command, and make her nest on high? She dwelleth and abideth on the rock, upon the crag of the rock, and the strong place.

Eagles walk with eagles. They live separately from other animals. Eagles don't fly with turkey or chickens. What makes eagles to live separate from other animals? Part of the reasons could be due to the fact that eagles notice the difference between them and other animals. Eagles don't mingle with animals that don't look like them. The Journey to the next level will require wisdom to notice the difference between you and people around. You are a child of covenant. You are different from the people of the world. You are not supposed to mingle with people that don't share the same belief with you. If you do, they will turn your heart from the living God and lure you into principles that will abort the journey to the next level. Also eagles separate themselves from other animals because they notice that no animal flies the way they do. Therefore to avoid delay or slow speed, eagles decide to fly alone.

There are people that will retard you in life if you journey with them. Avoid those people that will draw you back in the journey of life. Separate from mediocre. Furthermore, eagles separate from other animals in order to avoid burdens. For example if eagles decide to fly with animals that are naturally slower than them, they will need to assist them to fly at a higher altitude. Those animals will drain the energy of the eagles. There are people that will drain your limited resources. They will turn themselves into liability in your life. Such people will become a burden. The Journey to the next level will require that you avoid people that will add no value to your life otherwise they will become liabilities to you.

Avoid people that only always look unto you for financial assistance, advice, counsel, encouragement and motivation. Such people only take from you but have nothing to add to your life. They can't lift you up when you are down neither can they strengthen you when you are weak.

11. EAGLES FLY TOWARDS HEAVEN

Whenever there is danger on earth, eagles fly towards heaven for security. If a bush is burning or the earth quakes, eagles fly towards heaven for safety. In your journey to the next level, you must learn how to look unto heaven whenever challenges come. When situations go wrong; look unto heaven for intervention. Always put your confidence in God in heaven.

> **PSALMS 121:1**
>
> I will lift up mine eyes unto the hills, from whence cometh my help.

> **PSALMS 123:1**
>
> Unto thee lift I up mine eyes, O thou that dwellest in the heavens.

The above bible verses state that help is available in heaven. When situations become challenging, pray unto God for intervention.

> **ISAIAH 41:13**
>
> For I the Lord thy God will hold thy right hand, saying unto thee, Fear not; I will help thee.

God has promised to help you but you must look unto Him for it. Avoid common error of making man your confidence; it will only leads to regret. One of the reasons why you must look unto God instead of man is because no one can understand you except God. In *1 Samuel 1:11*, Prophet Eli misinterpreted Hannah and called her a drunkard. He could not understand why she was praying aggressively early in the day; but God who understands her answered her prayer in that year. Seek God who understands what you are facing. Pray to God who knows all things about you and your situations. Avoid seeking human help because everyman has his own race to run and they all have their own challenges also. May God give you strength to resist the temptation of making man your hope in Jesus name.

12. EAGLES RENEW STRENGTH

When an eagle grows old and the wings become worn out, it will go to the mountain and use its mouth to pluck out the old wings and feathers. After this, new wings and feathers grow out. The strength is renewed. Eagles rejuvenate. Renewal is necessary because the old can no longer meet the demand of the day. The anointing of yesterday will not be enough for the new day. Everything in life is changing and you will need to change so as to fit into the new day. You will soon discover that the knowledge of yesterday can't handle the challenges of today. You will need to constantly renew your knowledge about your career, job, dream, vision and other vital organs of your destiny. Even the devil changes his strategies to fit into the changing nature of man. Renew your knowledge. There are new books being written regularly with new inventions. There are new ideas and ways of handling events of life that keep on coming into our world regularly. Regularly update your knowledge. Similarly, you may need to renew your thinking pattern. *Romans 12:2*, says that there is a need for renewal of mind. You may need to change the way you see things in order to advance to the next level. Start thinking positively and begin to evaluate events around you in the light of the word of God. Similarly, there may be a need for a change of attitude. The old ways of reacting to situation may need to change.

The Israelites lived as slaves for over 400 years in Egypt. They had stayed too long in slavery such that they had fully developed the attitude of slaves. Slaves love to murmur behind their master. Slaves can never be satisfied as long as they remain slaves. Unfortunately when the Israelites were liberated from Egypt, they did not understand that they were no longer slaves but now sons and daughters of the living God. Though they were now free, their attitude was still of slaves not freed people. They eventually died in the wilderness. If you notice that negative situations around you remain unchanged, it may be a sign that a change of approach and methods is needed. Renew your styles and try new ways of doing things.

> **MARK 2:22**
>
> And no man putteth new wine into old bottles: else the new wine doth burst the bottles, and the wine is spilled, and the bottles will be marred: but new wine must be put into new bottles.

The above verse implies that the new should go with the new and vice-versa. A new approach in a new day will yield positive results.

> **PSALMS 92:10**
>
> But my horn shalt thou exalt like the horn of a unicorn: I shall be anointed with fresh oil.

The above Bible verse states that help is available to renew your strength. Fresh anointing is available from God if you can seek for it. May God renew your strength and give you fresh revelation for the new day in Jesus name.

PRAYER

Father, replace every weakness inside of me with your strength.

Father, use all my limitations for your own glory in Jesus name.

Father, open the 'eye of my mind' to identify enemies of my destinies in Jesus name.

Father, anoint me afresh and take me above all limitation of life.

Father, let every source that drains strength out of me dry today speedily in Jesus name.

Father, grant me supernaturally accelerated promotion in all that I lay my hands on in Jesus name.

Father, let every magnet inside of me that attract evil die today in Jesus name.

I build the walls of fire of God around all my dreams and visions in Jesus name.

I receive in abundance all resources that I need to finish well and strong all my plans in Jesus name.

I decree that I shall have breakthrough and not breakdown in all my ways in Jesus name.

CHAPTER 7

PRESS ON

> **PHILIPPIANS 3:12-14**
>
> Not that I have already attained, or am already perfected; but I press on, that I may lay hold of that for which Christ Jesus has also laid hold of me. Brethren, I do not count myself to have apprehended; but one thing I do, forgetting those things which are behind and reaching forward to those things which are ahead, I press toward the goal for the prize of the upward call of God in Christ Jesus. Therefore let us, as many as are mature, have this mind; and if in anything you think otherwise, God will reveal even this to you. Nevertheless, to the degree that we have already attained, let us walk by the same rule, let us be of the same mind.

From the above Paul declared that He is pressing on in order to lay hold of that for which Christ laid hold for him. You have to behave like Paul by pressing on towards the mark line irrespective of the opposition or prevailing circumstances. You have to press on against all odds, frustration, opposition, threat, disappointment, rejection, mockery or hatred. You have to behave like an athlete or runner who stretches every muscle as he runs towards the mark line. The journey to the next level will not be accomplished without identifying things to ignore in order to grasp the ultimate crown.

What are the things you need to ignore in your journey to the next level?

IGNORE ALL THAT IS BEHIND AND FOCUS ON ALL THAT IS AHEAD

In *Philippians 3:13,* Paul forgot those things which were behind him and he reached forward towards those things which were before him. If you give chance to things behind you, they are capable of holding you down. Example of things behind you may include:

1. Past Failure

The Devil knows you can't change your past so he wants to continually tie you to your past failure so that you can get distracted. In *Luke 5:3-6* Peter has to put his past failure behind him in order to follow divine instruction from Jesus. When Jesus asked him to launch out into the deep, the Devil reminded him of his past failure (all efforts he had made before Jesus came but with no result).

Many have become prisoners of their past failures and have lost confidence to move on in life. If you want to get to the next level you have to learn how to move on irrespective of the number of times you have failed. You have to consider every failed attempt as an opportunity to try again.

2. Mockers

There are people who have rejoiced over your past failure before and they are still rejoicing and mocking you when they see you continue on your journey. The only thing that will shut their mouth is your victory; so don't try to pay them any attention. In *1 Samuel 1:6* Peninnah was mocking Hannah because of her barrenness but Hannah ignored her and kept the fire of faith burning in her life.

When she gave birth to Samuel, Peninnah automatically shut her mouth up. It is the victory that closes the mouths of mockers, not by replying them. When your vision speaks, those who have been prophesying failure concerning it accept they were wrong. Don't spend time to reply your mockers because you may be delayed and miss your success. Don't miss the train!

3. Past Glory

Your past achievement can tie you down. If you want to live on past glory, you may be distracted in facing the present challenges.

In *Philippians 3:3-7,* Paul mentioned his undeniable attributes and personal accomplishments concerning himself. Despite all he had achieved as an expert in Jewish law and custom he put it aside and followed a new vision from heaven. He did not allow his noble background to tie him down. He moved and associated with the people that would not have come near him if not for a new life in Christ. Your journey to the next level may dispossess you of certain things you were used to. These may include old friends or certain possessions. Move on without raising the question as to why the former days were better than these days; as it written in *Ecclesiastes 7:10*. If you keep on the fight, you will win a better victory than the past.

> **ECCLESIASTES 7:10**
>
> Do not say, "Why were the former days better than these?" For you do not inquire wisely concerning this.

4. Past Disappointments

If you want to be thinking about disappointments in life and from friends and relatives, you will lose hope in the future. If you keep on thinking about people who have disappointed you in the past, you will miss the help of people that God will bring on your way for tomorrow's success. Stop thinking about people that were supposed to have helped you in the past but refused to do so.

In *John 5: 1-9*, there was a sick man at the pool of Bethesda who had been there for many years with no one to help him to jump into the pool for healing. He was trying to explain to Jesus that he has no one to help him. This suggests that he believed that his relatives and those capable of helping him did not render help and that was why he was still in that situation, but Jesus was not interested in the story because that had nothing to contribute to the healing the man needed. Don't let unforgiveness and bitterness bring complication into your journey.

Keep focusing on what is ahead. The fulfilment is ahead. The crown of victory is ahead. The joy of success is ahead. Keep motivating yourself with the gains that are ahead of you.

IGNORE THE ADVICE TO QUIT

When you launch out into the journey to the next level the enemy may cleverly surround you with people that will remind you of your limitations, lack of resources and other inadequacies. This is an attempt from the pit of hell to frustrate your vision. Don't listen to such evil advisers. Live above the opinions of men.

In *1 Samuel 17:32-37*, King Saul reminded David of his inexperience, limitation and the strength of his opponent. He told him that Goliath, was an experienced fighter and that it was not advisable for David to face such a great fighter. To King Saul, David had no chance of success, but David who knew his God Ignored the evil advice. David pressed on not in his own power but in the name of God (*1 Samuel 17:45*).

IGNORE THE THREAT TO QUIT

There are situations and people that may threaten you and your vision. This is an attempt to force you to quit. In *Acts 4:16-20*, the Disciples were warned to quit their divine assignment-never to use the name of Jesus again, but they refused to quit. At this stage they had only made a crippled man to walk. They had not done many wonders. They had not been raising the dead. Peter's shadow had not been used to heal the sick. The Devil was seriously afraid of their future performance, so, he wanted to force them out of their ministry before they went deeper. In *Acts 4:29*, Disciples prayed for boldness instead of quitting. When you launch out on your journey, hell can predict how far you can go for they know that you can do all things through Christ that strengthens you, so they organize threats through human agents. Resist the Devil and all his cohorts and they will flee from you. Press on.

IGNORE ALL THAT HINDERS AND FOCUS ON ALL THAT HELP

As you progress on your journey, hell brings various things that can hinder you but God will always bring those things that can help you. God is always ahead of every situation for He exists before all things. Let helpers motivate you while you ignore discouragement from the agents of hindrances.

In *Nehemiah 4:1-3*, the Devil brings people to hinder the work of Nehemiah but there were other good people that God brought ahead of the enemy to work tirelessly with Nehemiah. There are things that hinder but there are things that help. There are people that hinder and there are people that help. There are people that pull down and there are people that lift up. There are things that demoralise and there are things that motivate. There are resources you don't have but there are resources that you have. You can use what you have to get what you don't have. Spend your time on things that promote your journey instead of wasting time to address people that are abusing you. Shift your focus to things that help. Make the right choice.

IGNORE THE LOSSES AND FOCUS ON THE GAINS

Life is about give and take. Something has to be lost for something to be gained. The Journey to the next level will not be accomplished without losing certain things. People that became great in the Bible had to lose something in order for them to gain what God had promised them.

> **HEBREWS 11:23-7**
>
> By faith Moses, when he was born, was hidden three months by his parents, because they saw he was a beautiful child; and they were not afraid of the king's command.
>
> By faith Moses, when he became of age, refused to be called the son of Pharaoh's daughter, choosing rather to suffer affliction with the people of God than to enjoy the passing pleasures of sin, esteeming the reproach of Christ greater riches than the treasures in Egypt; for he looked to the reward.
>
> By faith he forsook Egypt, not fearing the wrath of the king; for he endured as seeing Him who is invisible.

The above states that Moses lost the enjoyment of Egypt in order to fulfil his calling. He preferred to lose the treasures of Egypt because he understood the gains ahead. Sometimes, what it is required to fulfil a vision may be so great that the person may decide not to pursue it but you have to be determined to pay the required price. For Abraham to inherit the land God gave him, he had to lose his old associates in his home country. When God called him out in *Genesis 12*, he knew he would never see some of his old associates again. He would also lose forever all his landed property, yet he obeyed God for he could see the gain ahead.

Let the gains motivate you and press on irrespective of the costs.

IGNORE THE VISIBLE AND FOCUS ON THE INVISIBLE

> **2 CORINTHIANS 5:7**
>
> For we walk by faith, not by sight.

The above scripture states that we walk by faith and not by sight. To walk by faith means to see the unseen and to walk by sight means to see the things which are physical. By sight, we see failure but by faith, we see success. By sight, we may see death but by faith we can see life. By sight our dreams are not achievable but by faith they are achievable. Only those that can see beyond the physical will be able to reach the next level.

If you will complete this journey, don't be moved by what you see but by the unseen promises of God. Don't be moved by what you hear but by what the word of God says.

In *2 Kings 6:15-17*, the Servant of Elisha could not see the provision God had made for their protection, so, fear gripped his mind. Elisha was bold even in the face of the enemies' attack because he could see beyond the physical.

It is time for you to start discerning spiritual matters from God's perspective and see beyond what men can see. Press on for it is well.

IGNORE THE PRESSURE OF TOMORROW'S NEEDS

God will not give details though, He may show the end from the beginning. He brings into physical the provision he has made only when the time of need comes. Learn to live for today. Don't wait for everything to be ready before you launch out. You launch out when you have what is needed to start the journey and as time goes on, things begin to fall into places at the appointed time. It is what you need now that God has provided and when the time for tomorrow's needs arises, God will make them available. In *Genesis 22:7-8*, Isaac asked Abraham about the lamb for sacrifice but Abraham replied him that God would provide. At this time, there was no need for the lamb because the situation that would require the lamb had not come. When the need for the lamb came, God provided. Many die unfulfilled because they were waiting for perfect situations before launching out.

> **ECCLESIASTES 11:4**
>
> He who observes the wind will not sow, and he who regards the clouds will not reap.

The above suggests that he that waits for perfect situation before starting a good thing will never achieve anything in his life. Ignore the concern for tomorrow's needs and press on. In *Psalm 118:24*, David declared that this is the day the Lord has made he will rejoice and be glad in it. He did not want the concern for tomorrow's needs to rob him of the enjoyment of today. Press on. Leave tomorrow for God and continue with your journey.

FINAL WORD

NO CONTEST! NO VICTORY!!

There has to be a contest before there can be a victor. You can't have a battle without an opposition. It is the principle of God's kingdom that there must be a battle before a winner can be declared. It is, therefore, not strange that you face what you are facing on your journey to the next level. No cross, no crown.

> **REVELATION 12:7-12**
>
> And war broke out in heaven: Michael and his angels fought with the dragon; and the dragon and his angels fought, but they did not prevail, nor was a place found for them in heaven any longer. So the great dragon was cast out, that serpent of old, called the Devil and Satan, who deceives the whole world; he was cast to the earth, and his angels were cast out with him. Then I heard a loud voice saying in heaven, "Now salvation, and strength, and the kingdom of our God, and the

> power of His Christ have come, for the accuser of our brethren, who accused them before our God day and night, has been cast down. And they overcame him by the blood of the Lamb and by the word of their testimony, and they did not love their lives to the death. Therefore rejoice O heavens, and you who dwell in them! Woe to the inhabitants of the earth and the sea! For the devil has come down to you, having great wrath, because he knows that he has a short time."

The above reveals that there was a battle in heaven between the forces of darkness and those of light. The battle is still on today. There will never be a peace accord between the forces of evil and good. The good news is that the forces of good always prevail over the forces of evil. It is a matter of time, good will overcome evil. No matter how hard the enemy tries, he remains a loser.

Every plan or journey that is of God will face the test. The kingdom of darkness will be allowed to oppose it for a short time in order to prove if it was of God or man. Let nothing move you.

He that began a good work in you will complete it. When God arises, His enemies are scattered. Today, God will arise for your sake in Jesus name. Enjoy your journey.

PRAYER

- *Father, help me to always act, think and speak as a blessed one. Let me see myself and the situation around me as you see them. Let me manifest the mind of Christ in all my ways in Jesus name*

- *Father, deliver my soul from lying lips and from a deceitful tongue. Separate me from trouble makers and remove terror and fear from my life in Jesus name*

- *Father, be an enemy to my enemies and show Yourself as an adversary to my adversaries in Jesus name. Afflict those that want to afflict me*

- *Father, let every gate of hell be lifted up for my sake and cause me to enter into my inheritance fully in Jesus name.*

- *Father, destroy every work of the devil in my life today in Jesus name. Break every manner of yoke in my life and make me to walk straight.*

- *Father, make me unstoppable and unconquerable in all my ways. Let no man be able to stand against me on my way. Collapse the wall of Jericho confronting me with your command in Jesus name*

- *Father, multiply your anointing on me. Renew my strength and anoint me afresh in Jesus name. Grant me divine enablement to operate my life.*

- *Father, give me boldness and understanding to use the authority You have vested in me as Your child. Whatever I decree let it be established in Jesus name.*

- *God of direction, direct me on the way to go. Order my steps and lead me away from destruction in Jesus name.*

- *Father, frustrate every gang-up (both physical and spiritual) against me. Wherever my name is mentioned, let the blood of Jesus answer for me*

- *Every spirit agent or structure or voices representing me for evil purposes in any place - Father, destroy their mission. Frustrate the activities of the spirit of impersonation in my life.*

- *Let everything that is divinely mine reach me in Jesus name.*

- *Father, fight all my battles for me and grant me victory in Jesus name.*

BOOKS FROM THE SAME AUTHOR

The New Creature

Words That Heal

Building a Glorious Home

The Winning Dose

This book, and all other books from the same author, are available at Christian bookstores and distributors worldwide.
They can also be obtained through online retail partners such as Amazon or by contacting the author on the address below.

Contacts:

21-23 Stokescroft

Bristol BS1 3PY

United Kingdom

E-mail:

kkasali@yahoo.com

www.ingramcontent.com/pod-product-compliance
Lightning Source LLC
Chambersburg PA
CBHW072056290426
44110CB00014B/1711